# LEADING TEAMS

by David Pardey

Editor Claire Nash

Published by

# ilm

Stowe House, Netherstowe
Lichfield, Staffs WS13 6TJ
Tel: 01543 251346
Fax: 01543 266811
Email: leadingteams@i-l-m.com

ILM is part of the City & Guilds Group

ISBN 1 902475 02 X

Writer       David Pardey
Editor       Claire Nash
Designer     Sarah Dobinson
Illustrator  Mark Hackett

# Contents

# Foreword

## by John Adair

There is a revolution under way. We are moving rapidly from old-style management – downsizing, command and control, bossing – to the concept of business leadership.

It emerges that there are three key levels of leadership in any organisation or enterprise: *strategic* (the whole outfit); *operational* (a significant part of the whole, with more than one team reporting to you); and *team* – the basic small group of around ten people.

Success lies in excellence at all levels – and teamwork between them.

The trouble with most organisations today is that they are focussing a disproportionate amount of time and resources in trying to improve leadership at the strategic level (not very effectively, but that's another matter), and neglecting the team leadership level almost entirely.

This is nonsense really, because it is the *team* that delivers product or service, creates the delighted customer and is the matrix for creative and innovative thinking.

You can see why I welcome *Leading Teams* – a simple, clear and practical book on how to become a team leader.

Team leadership is an area where intellectually we have made some real breakthroughs in the past five decades; notably in identifying clearly the *role* of the team leader and the chief *functions* that a team leader has responsibility for – which doesn't mean that he or she undertakes them all on his or her own.

David Pardey wisely grounds his book on this core of knowledge.

But I mustn't stand any longer between you and *Leading Teams*. It will take you far along the path of becoming an effective team leader. My warm good wishes are with you for the journey.

*John Adair*

# Introduction

Teams are an increasingly important feature of working life, but not all teams work as well as they should. Some 'teams' are not true teams at all. Some work processes do not lend themselves well to team working, and neither do some people. But where true teams can be created and nurtured, the opportunity exists for getting real benefits all round.

There are not many ways in which organisations can achieve genuine 'wins' for all, but team working is one. Such 'wins' for an organisation can include the achievement of its goals, reduced costs, improved quality, lower staff turnover, fewer accidents, fewer days lost through sickness and better staff morale and motivation. 'Wins' for customers or service users can be because they are offered better goods or services, or lower prices. Employees can 'win' through better pay or more secure employment, more say in the way that things are done and a more personally enriching experience at work.

Effective and efficient teams do not come without a cost, of course. There are likely to be financial costs incurred in reorganising working practices and training people, but the main 'cost' is probably the hard work and commitment needed to create and support the development of teams. Most importantly, the organisation needs to dedicate itself to creating team leaders who can get the best out of their team members. Without effective team leaders, there is far less chance of achieving all that team working can offer.

*Leading Teams* is designed to help team leaders to achieve all-round benefits from team working. The book is written for people who have already taken on a team leadership role and for those who are about to do so. It assumes that the organisation has already assessed that team working is an appropriate method and is committed to working through teams.

The book will also be valuable to people taking the Institute of Leadership and Management's (ILM's) Level 2 Certificate in Team Leading. It covers the content of the Certificate and most of the units in the national occupational standards – the National Vocational Qualification (NVQ) and Scottish Vocational Qualification (SVQ) – in team leading.

*Leading Teams* takes a step-by-step approach, with each chapter building on the previous one. Even so, readers can just as easily dip into the book at any point to explore a particular issue.

All subjects have their own special language, and organisational management and team leadership are no exceptions. Jargon has been kept to a minimum, but key words and phrases of particular use to team leaders are highlighted in blue in the chapters and the index.

Every chapter finishes with a summary of the most practicable learning points. There is also a review section to help readers to consider what might work best for them in their particular workplaces, particular jobs and with specific team members.

The chapters are grouped into four sections covering the critical aspects of team working and the team leader role.

Section One outlines what teams are, how they work and why they are so important. Section Two discusses the role of the team leader and the skills that team leaders need to perform effectively. A key part of the team leader role is being able to work effectively with people, and Section Three deals with the team leader's relationship with others, in particular, everyday communication. Section Four deals with the operational issues involved in team working and leadership, including health and safety and ways to continuously improve the team's performance.

At the end of the book, in 'Acknowledgments', are the full details of the sources of the ideas and research mentioned in the chapters that have been omitted for easier reading. Another section, entitled 'Further help', provides suggestions for additional sources of ideas and practical help.

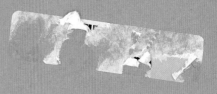

# Teams and team working

Working in teams offers real benefits, but these do not appear by magic. It takes hard work, commitment and understanding to turn groups of people into real and effective teams. Only through understanding what makes the best teams, can you become an effective team leader.

Teams are not just groups of people working together. Real teams have some structure and organisation. The members of teams have different parts to play in getting the team's work done and doing so effectively. Team members also need to feel that they belong to the team, and others must recognise them as being a part of the particular team.

Members of the most effective, high-performing teams are able to accept responsibility for their work, making decisions among themselves and sharing power. Team members feel accountable for their actions as a team and regard the team's performance as being more important than the achievement of their own individual goals. As a result, they are able to take the lead in improving quality, controlling costs and helping one another to develop and improve themselves.

This section describes what teams are, how they work, what they are capable of achieving and how team leaders can help their colleagues to get the best from the team.

# 1 | What are teams?

## Introduction

Teams are found in a wide range of organisations in the public sector (such as the health service, education and local government), in the private sector (business) and in the voluntary sector (charities and the like). Working in teams – or calling groups of people 'teams' – has become popular over the last couple of decades. But are all the groups that are called teams really teams, and are some work groups actually teams without being called teams?

In this chapter you will find out what teams are and how they differ from work groups. You will also learn about different types of teams in the workplace, the importance of having the right set of skills and of being organised to take advantage of them. You will also find out about the importance of agreeing clear goals for the team and its members to ensure that you get the best out of your team.

## What is a team?

It's easy enough to call a group of people 'a team', but calling them a team doesn't make them a team. Being a team is more than simply working together or being given a label. In fact, some teams don't necessarily *physically* work together at all but spend most of their time working on their own or with other people who are not in the team. And there are plenty of work groups called teams that are not teams at all, just as there are some real teams that are not necessarily called teams.

> **Example 1** | A company has ten sales people who are supervised by a national sales manager. They work from home and visit customers in their sales regions. Every three months they meet for two days to review sales, learn about new products or promotions and so on. They are called the *national sales team*.
>
> **Example 2** | A council has six district offices, each with specialists from its housing, environmental services, social services and financial departments. The receptionist identifies the needs of the residents and directs them to the appropriate specialist officer. Residents with multiple problems see a different officer in turn. The district officers are called the *neighbourhood team*.
>
> **Example 3** | A plastics company is organised into 'cells', each cell making products for particular customers. The people in each cell are responsible for the whole production process. They sample production regularly to check quality, do simple maintenance on machines and can change the tools used in the machines without calling in specialist fitters. The people in each cell are called the *cell team*.

Are all three examples on the previous page really teams? What is a team? There are quite a few definitions that could be used: you'll find just four below. Full information on who said what is given on page 150.

"A team is a small number of people with complementary skills who are committed to a common purpose, performance goals and approach for which they hold themselves mutually accountable."

"Structured groups of people working on defined common goals that require co-ordinated interactions to accomplish certain tasks."

"A group of people with different skills and different tasks, who work together on a common project, service, or goal, with a meshing of functions and mutual support."

"A group of people organized to work together."

What these definitions have in common are the following four key points:

- teams are groups of people
- teams perform a range of tasks requiring different skills
- teams are organised
- teams have their own goals, for which team members are jointly responsible.

We will look at these four points in turn.

## Teams are made up of groups of people

This is probably obvious as you cannot be a team of one! But not all *groups* of people are a team. A team is a special type of group, one that has all the other characteristics as well. An important question is, how big a group should it be? Are there upper and lower limits on the size of a team, and if so, what are they?

Management consultants Jon Katzenbach and Douglas Smith say that there is an upper limit so that teams should consist of between 2 and 25 people, but ideally fewer than ten. They argue that as teams get larger, it becomes harder for people to meet, get to know one another, discuss things and reach agreement. In fact, as teams get larger, they break into smaller groups of two or more sub-teams.

This makes sense. Where in your workplace could you get 20 or 30 people together at any one time? Keeping the group smaller is one way of ensuring that people can physically meet, which is one of the things that teams need to do.

Even if a larger team could get together, it would be hard for everyone to have a say in a discussion. Seven people could each speak for three or four minutes in a half hour meeting, but 25 would be lucky to have a minute each. And there would be problems in getting to know one another well, so that the group would break into cliques – people with similar ideas and attitudes. The result is likely to be constant arguments as each clique tries to have its say.

If large groups are likely to be a problem, what about small ones? Having different people working together brings different ideas, different skills and different points of view. Very few of these benefits are available with only two or three people, so a team is likely to be a group of at least five people but fewer than a dozen.

## Teams perform a range of tasks requiring different skills

As you'll see from the box below, there tend to be three main types of team in organisations:

- management teams
- task, ad hoc or project teams that have been put together for a particular purpose
- operational or production teams.

Management teams These can be the 'top' management ('senior' management or 'executive' team) or managers at the same level (departmental or account managers, for example). They have similar responsibilities for different areas of operations and, as a team, they co-ordinate decisions and ensure the smooth running of the organisation.

Task, ad hoc or project teams These are teams set up for a specific purpose with a fixed lifespan. Once they have achieved their goal, they are dissolved. They can be formed at various levels, from groups of senior managers or specialists (supervising a major investment or a takeover, for example), through cross-functional teams with different types of expertise (perhaps to develop new products), to operational or production groups (identifying and resolving quality problems, perhaps).

Operational teams These are the teams that *Leading Teams* is mainly about. They make the goods or provide the services that an organisation exists to make or provide. Operational teams carry out the organisation's main activities or 'operations'. Examples of such teams include teams in a factory on a production line or in a cell or zone; teams in a sales office or call centre; the crew of a fire appliance, a tank or an aeroplane; the pickers and loaders in a warehouse; or the waiters in a restaurant.

In a team the members all contribute different skills that enable a wide range of tasks to be completed. The tasks are approached collectively, and each person is prepared to help others in the team and to learn new skills from the others. In contrast, members of a work *group* tend to keep to their own areas of specialism, focussing on one task or combination of tasks. The skills people contribute tend to be of two main types:

- task-related
- team-related.

Task-related skills are needed for the main tasks that someone undertakes. They include financial or marketing skills (in a management team), engineering or design skills (in a project team), and customer relations or administrative skills (in an operational team). Team-related skills are needed for the smooth working of the team. We'll look at these skills in more detail later in the book, but they include being good at solving problems, encouraging people to contribute ideas, or making sure that tasks have been completed. They also include leading the team.

Team members may have the same set of task-related skills, but they are not always to the same standard. Recognising who is best at which task, or part of a task, helps people to play to their strengths. The most successful or high-performing teams tend to have team members who have developed new skills by learning from one another. Such 'multi-skilling' helps the team to be *flexible*, so that team members can turn their hands (and brains) to more than one task or can substitute for another team member. The level of skill is obviously important as well – being multi-skilled doesn't just mean being capable of doing tasks, it means being *highly capable*.

## Team skills in action

Sports teams often exhibit high levels of skill coupled with flexibility. The players play in positions that require them to perform in different ways, but if one player is injured, the team's players may have to take up different positions. The better the players, the more likely it is that they can perform effectively in more than one position.

A team in the workplace is much the same. Different tasks require different skills and abilities, and the higher the skill level of each team member, the better the team will perform. If one team member is away sick or on holiday, the remaining team members are able to cover for a missing team member, performing the tasks to the same standard. A team member's absence will have little or no effect in the short term.

## Teams are organised

A work *group* may not need to be very organised because the members work on their own. In contrast, a *team* needs organisation because the members are inter-dependent, and what one member does affects other members of the team. Without some sort of organisation, the work of different team members would not be co-ordinated and the chance would be lost to make the best of everyone's specific skills.

For a team leader, organising the team is a major responsibility, although team leaders do not have to do this on their own. The more developed the team is, the more able it is to organise its work collectively. The team leader's role is not to do the organising, but to make sure that the team is well organised. You'll learn more about this in Chapter 2.

## Joint responsibility for goals

A working *group* contains individuals with their own particular goals or objectives. However, a *team* has *collective* goals. Although team members may also have their own individual goals, these are all based on the team's collective goals. This is probably the most important distinction between a working group and team. For example, a team may have the goal of halving the number of faulty products on a production line. Individual members may have specific individual goals, such as checking each component before fitting it or monitoring the temperature of a particular process. Each of these individual goals contributes to the overall goal that the team members are collectively responsible for achieving.

Goals help to focus the team on its responsibilities: they provide a mechanism for reviewing how well it is performing and they can encourage the team to perform to a higher standard. In Chapter 5 we'll look at team and individual goals in more detail.

## Summary

- There are three main types of teams – management, task (or ad hoc or project) and operational teams. *Leading Teams* focusses on operational teams, which are responsible for producing the goods and services an organisation provides.

- Real teams are more than just *groups* of people.

- Real teams are able to perform a range of tasks requiring different skills (both task-related and team-related).

- Real teams need to be organised to ensure that they make the best of these skills.

- Real teams have their own goals, for which the team's members are jointly responsible.

## Review your learning

Look back at the three examples on page 2.

- Which of these groups would you call a team, and why?

- What kind of team is it/are they?

In a team the members all contribute different skills that enable a wide range of tasks to be completed.

# 2 | How teams work

## Introduction

Teams are groups of people with different skills working together in an organised way to achieve their goals. Over the next few chapters you'll find out more about the characteristics of teams and why they are so important. This includes looking at the skills team members need, how they are organised and how having goals affects the performance of the team and the individuals in it. In this chapter you will find out more about how teams are organised and the effect this has on the way that people work. This includes looking at team structures, the rules governing the team and its members' work roles and relationships. It also introduces you to team 'cultures' and the effect these have on performance.

## Team structures

One of the things we all take for granted, wherever we go, whatever we do, is that there is some form of organisation. Organisation means that people know what other people can be expected to do or how other people can be expected to act or treat you. Organisation is about:

* rules
* roles
* relationships.

These define the team's structure. Organisation is also about 'culture' – team members' attitudes, customs and expectations – and the team's 'norms'. We'll look at these ideas in more detail to see how they affect the way that teams work.

## Structures involve rules

Rules control what people are permitted to do. For example, in soccer only the goalkeeper may handle the ball. In a netball team members must stand still when holding the ball. The football game where all players can handle the ball becomes rugby, netball becomes basketball if the players can move around while holding the ball.

Rules also help to define teams at work. Rules are used to do two things – to state what people must do, and what they must *not* do. Rules that say what you *must* do tend to be much more controlling than those that say what you must *not* do. A rule that says you must not touch the ball with your hands allows you to touch it with any other part of your body. A rule that says you must stand with both feet on the ground means just that – you must not move your feet.

Teams that are told precisely what they *must* do have *less* power over their work than teams that are told only what they must *not* do. Teams governed by 'must *not*' rules have the freedom (within reason) to do other things and have more power over their work. Teams like this are empowered. We'll come back to empowerment in Chapter 3 because it is an important idea in team working.

## Case study

Leonard and Willcox produces plastic components for a leading manufacturer of domestic power tools (the customer). Both companies have teams that deal directly with each other about the quality of the products and the quantity and times of deliveries. The delivery driver from Leonard and Willcox takes the components straight onto the manufacturer's production line. While there, he is told which components are needed in the next delivery. He phones the team at Leonard and Willcox, so that they can make the order ready, and he keeps a record of orders and deliveries using a PDA (personal digital assistant). This information is downloaded onto the Leonard and Willcox computer at the end of each day. This system works well because both companies trust their teams. The rules for both sets of teams allow the team members to vary the precise details of what is delivered according to the customer's current requirements. There are limits to how much they can vary what is supplied, but within those limits team members have the freedom to make their own decisions.

## Structures involve roles

Roles are what people are expected to do in a team. Team roles vary but there are some roles that are more common than others, including the role of team leader. Leaders of operational teams are part of the team and usually have similar jobs to everyone else in the team. What they also do is to:

- help the team to agree its goals

- act as a bridge between the team, its managers and other teams

- deal first with any problems that may occur

- generally make sure that the team is doing what it is meant to be doing, as well as it can.

But the team leader is not the only role in a team. There are other roles that may exist, and some of these are listed in the box opposite. These roles help the team members to do their jobs well, safely and to make the best use of the resources, like tools and equipment, materials, components and the power, heat and light teams need (see also Chapter 19). These roles are task-focussed, which means that they are concerned with ensuring that the team's tasks are performed well.

Team leaders fulfil some of the roles shown in the box on page 10 (in some cases all of them), but they don't have to. One of the benefits of team working is that each team member can try out and take on different roles. This helps team members to

> One of the benefits of team working is that each team member can try out and take on different roles.

understand what is important and why things are done the way they are. It also gives people more interest in their jobs and motivates them to work well.

## Team roles

**Training, buddying or coaching.**

**Monitoring product or service quality.**

**Maintaining equipment.**

**Monitoring health and safety.**

**Liaising with suppliers.**

**Liaising with customers.**

**Organising tools and equipment.**

**Controlling materials and consumable items.**

## Team-focussed roles

There can be other roles in the team, roles that are team-focussed. These help the team to improve and work better as a team. These may be unofficial roles, such as the team joker, the team astrologer and the team social secretary, but they can be just as important.

Letting people play these social roles helps members to feel part of a team. Social roles are like oil on a moving part, they lubricate it and stop friction. However, team leaders must prevent social roles from taking over so that they do not delay work.

## Personalities

There is another way of looking at team roles – the way that people's personalities contribute to how the team works. Personality is about how friendly, outgoing and enthusiastic people are; how careful and controlled they are about detail; how positive and optimistic they are about what is likely to happen; and how open they are to new ideas.

It pays to have a variety of personalities, because they can each contribute something to the way the team works. Having someone who is always keen to try new things is helped if there's also someone who is cautious and says, 'Let's just try it out in a small way first and see if it works'.

There are lots of different ways of testing for personality types and seeing how they contribute to effective team working. One that is widely used was developed by the British academic R Meredith Belbin. He describes eight different team roles, which are summarised on page 5. They might give you an insight into your own and your team members' role preferences. This can help you to think about how you work with other people.

## Belbin's team roles

Implementers **Keen to get things done, are not easily distracted and show common sense, although they can be a little unoriginal.**

Co-ordinators **Good at seeing the best in, and getting the best out of, other people. Generally well respected by the rest of the team.**

Shapers **Keen to get things moving, are competitive, can be argumentative and don't easily give up.**

Completer-finisher **Good at making sure things are finished and loose ends are tidied up. They prefer to do things themselves rather than leave it to others.**

Plants **Imaginative and keen to try out new things, they are good at coming up with innovative ideas, but not so good at accepting criticism.**

Resource investigators **Good at accepting other people's ideas and working with them to make them happen, and finding whatever is needed to do so.**

Monitor-evaluators **Cautious, reluctant to jump quickly to any decisions, but good at testing out ideas and checking things are being done properly.**

Team workers **Popular with the rest of the team and good with people, they make sure that everyone is pulling together in the same direction.**

## Structures involve relationships

Relationships are how individuals relate to, communicate with, have attitudes towards, influence or show behaviour towards one another. Most people move in several different groups, such as their families, friends, clubs or societies, as well as the people at work. They have different relationships with the people in all of these groups, and they generally know how to change the way they behave with the members of every group. Most relationships at work are more formal than those at home or with friends. There are some things you can do or say with friends that you know you wouldn't do or say at work.

### Hierarchical relationships in organisations

One important feature of relationships at work is the power or authority that certain people have over others – they have the power to tell people what to do. The more senior they are, the more power they generally have over more people. This is because most organisations have a hierarchical structure – the organisations have layers, or levels, of people whose job roles give them increasing power or control over the people in lower layers. In typical organisation charts, such as the one opposite, it is easy to see that some roles are shown at different levels. When the links between them are horizontal (ie. at the same level), then they have the same power as other jobholders at that level. If the links are vertical (ie. one above the other), then those in the higher levels have more power than the jobholders below them.

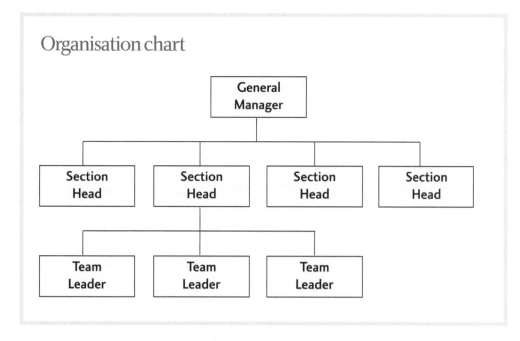

## Team hierarchies

Some teams have a hierarchy too, with some members being more powerful than others, perhaps because of their seniority or their age, or simply because they are the team leader's favourites. The most effective teams do not have hierarchies. Every member is equal, including the team leader. Being a team leader doesn't mean that you need to have or to use the power in order to control the team.

## Flat structures

Teams without hierarchies usually have flat structures (without the different levels shown on the organisation chart above). The relationships between people in the team are quite relaxed and friendly, which encourages openness and trust. It can also encourage people to take advantage. People in teams often like to socialise outside work and have fun together, which can help to build strong relationships. But it should not mean that when they are at work, work is an optional extra. A team leader needs to ensure that the emphasis at work is about getting the job done well. That's why clear goals at work are so useful – they give the team a focus, without the team leader having to keep tight control all the time.

## Culture

Team structures, rules, roles and relationships define one aspect of how teams work, but a workplace's 'culture' and 'norms' can also have a significant impact on team performance. **Culture** is very hard to define but very easy to see or recognise when you find yourself surrounded by another or unfamiliar culture. When you are abroad, you will be aware of obvious differences, such as language, types of food and the side of the road people must drive on. Other differences are more subtle.

People may differ in how they use or don't use first names when they meet someone for the first time, or the times that they work, eat, socialise and so on. Some of these differences reflect the rules, roles and relationships in their society, but the most significant difference is in the general way that people behave, think and act. This is their culture – what identifies them.

> ## easyJet
>
> **A distinctive feature of the low cost airline easyJet is the instantly recognisable, orange staff uniform. The company launched itself as being a very different airline to the others. The simple but bright uniforms contrast sharply with the tailored uniforms of many of the more traditional airline companies, and so emphasise a business approach that is informal, low cost and without frills.**

Management writer Marvin Bower once described culture as being 'the way things are around here'. Most organisations have their own culture. It may be a very busy, hard working, 'nose to the grindstone' way of doing things, or it may be a very relaxed, friendly, 'don't worry, it'll get done somehow' kind of culture. Organisational culture is formed by:

- attitudes (how people look at the world)

- customs (how people normally behave)

- expectations (what people expect others to do).

As teams develop, so they tend to develop their own culture. This can even mean developing their own:

- language (like nicknames for suppliers or customers)

- symbols (badges or emblems, or having their own team name)

- traditions (buying cream cakes for the team on your birthday).

In one insurance company all the call centre teams were named after different Scottish clans, each with their own little flags showing the clan tartan. Over time, some of the teams became more enthusiastic about their clans, researching them, wearing clothes with the clan tartan to work and selecting team mascots based on events in the clan's history.

## Culture creates norms

Norms are what the team regards as normal. People in a group have to get on together, to know the rules of the group, their different roles within it and how they relate to each other. Some of these are 'official', encouraged by the employer. Some are not. Most groups of people develop a common understanding of the right way to do things, and these are the group's norms. They reflect the team's culture, how team members are encouraged to behave, their attitudes and what they should expect from one other. Norms can affect how tasks are performed, the

> Norms encourage the team members to work together, to support one another and to feel a strong sense of belonging to the team.

speed at which people work and the standard of goods and services they produce. New team members are encouraged to share these norms, to behave in the same way, work at the same pace and generally conform. Norms encourage the team members to work together, to support one another and to feel a strong sense of belonging to the team.

As team leader, you should encourage those norms that help to improve efficiency and the quality of work and make the team happier and better motivated. But watch out for norms that make life easier for the team. This could mean avoiding more difficult tasks, or not trying very hard.

### Teams need to be able to accept non-conformity

Your most important responsibility in this context is to watch out for unfair pressure on anyone who doesn't conform to the team's norms. They can be made an outsider, miss out on team social activity and be left to do all the unpleasant jobs. This can even become discriminatory. In some workplaces, teams tend to consist of people who are all the same age, sex or ethnicity, and someone who is different can be made to feel excluded. This can also mean that the team accepts or even encourages the bullying of people who do not conform. We'll return to some of these issues later in the book, when we look in more detail at diversity and inclusivity in the workplace (in Chapter 16) and conflict (in Chapter 17).

## Summary

- Teams need a structure and organisation.

- Teams with few imposed rules tend to be more empowered.

- Team roles can be task-focussed, helping the team to perform its tasks better, or team-focussed, helping the team members to work better as a team.

- Relationships in teams are based less on hierarchy, but more on equality.

- Teams tend to create norms, defining what the team expects from its members. These can help the team to work together, but can also *exclude* people or make them feel pressured to conform.

## Review your learning

- How clear are the different roles in your team? Do you have *task* and *team* roles for team members to fill?

- What sort of culture does your team have? What attitudes, customs and expectations distinguish it from other teams?

- What norms does your team have? Do any of these prevent it from performing as well as you think it could?

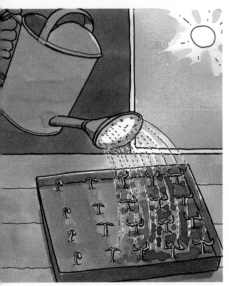

# 3 | Giving power to the team

## Introduction

A true team has the ability to make decisions about what it does and how it does it. This chapter looks at the power that teams gain and use when they have the authority to make decisions and to be accountable for those decisions. If teams are to take on this responsibility, they need to ensure that different team members know what their role is and what is expected of them. Teams that are able to accept this responsibility are on their way to becoming self-managing.

## Empowerment

**Empowerment** involves giving power to people. They are *empowered* when they have the authority to make decisions without having to ask permission. Many managers and team leaders believe that if they give other people more power it means that they have less. They think there is only a certain amount of power that is shared out across the organisation, so if someone gains, someone else loses.

This is true in physics. There is only so much mass, so if you give something to another person, then you have less. It is also true in economics. If you give away some of your money, you have less to spend yourself.

But personal power is different. Give power to someone and you don't lose it yourself. You still have the power because you can always take it back if someone misuses it.

## Delegation and power

The more power you give to people, the more you create. When you **delegate** a task or responsibility to someone, you entrust him or her to carry it out. By delegating responsibility to others, you give them the power to make decisions in your place. This adds to the total amount of power. An organisation that delegates power, by empowering teams and team leaders, becomes more powerful itself.

Empowering people allows them to make decisions, but it is only fair to do so if they have the confidence to make those decisions. One way of delegating power safely and fairly is by empowering teams, rather than individuals. Teams can share power and make collective decisions, which builds personal and team confidence. Team members also share the responsibility that comes with power.

If your employer gives you the power to make decisions because you are the team leader, don't feel that you have to hold on to it yourself. Share it with your team. The team members can help you to make better decisions, and they may take some of the weight off your shoulders. Another advantage of sharing decision-making is that it produces more ideas about what might be done, more knowledge and experience is available to inform the decisions, and there are more thoughts about the consequences.

People who make their own decisions are more committed to them. This means that they will work hard to ensure that the decisions are successful. Sharing power and responsibility creates better motivated teams and brings more chance of success. The downside is that decisions can take longer to make. Different ideas need to be explored, different points of view heard, and arguments can occur. The people with the loudest voices could sway the decisions, not the people with the best ideas or experience. As team leader, you need to enable all points of view to be aired, but without wasting time. You need to make sure that those who are hogging the limelight listen to the others. You also need to make sure that it isn't you who is hogging the limelight!

Finally, you need to know which decisions can be:

- made collectively

- delegated to individuals

- made by you or by someone more senior, such as your manager.

The criteria in the box below can help you.

## Sharing decisions

| Decisions best made collectively by the team | Decisions best made by individuals in the team (including the team leader, marked 'TL') | Decisions best made by someone more senior than team leader, or after consultation with such a person |
|---|---|---|
| **Those that affect everyone** | **Decisions in crises, emergencies and accidents** (TL) | **Those concerned with serious disciplinary or safety issues** |
| **Those requiring a wide range of experience, knowledge and ideas** | **Those with limited impact needing quick decisions** | **Those which have implications beyond the team** |
| **Those having long-term consequences for the team** | **Those affecting one person's work alone** | **Those which are clearly beyond the authority of the team or which the team leader feels uncertain about** |
| **Those that change how work is done** | **Those which are contentious, with strongly held but differing views** (TL) | |

## Accountability

One consequence of empowerment is that the responsibility involved also brings accountability – accounting for your actions to someone else. Having made a decision, you must accept the consequences and account for how well you used the power to those from whom the power was delegated. The power that is delegated down by senior managers is balanced by accountability going back up in the reverse direction. Responsibility combines delegated power (authority) and accountability for how you use it (see the diagram below).

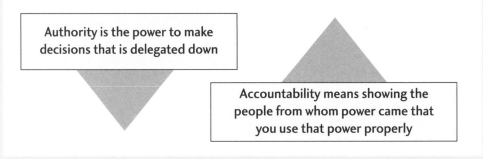

### Responsibility balances authority with accountability

**Authority is the power to make decisions that is delegated down**

**Accountability means showing the people from whom power came that you use that power properly**

There are many ways that accountability operates. It may be through monitoring or measuring the quantity or quality of your and your team's work. It may be through performance assessment or appraisal, when managers discuss teams' and team leaders' work and give them feedback on their performance. It may be through reporting on your performance, giving your own views on how you have performed. But there's no way of avoiding accountability, except by being completely powerless.

## Self-managed teams

When team members are allowed to make decisions about how they work, how they share tasks, even how they are rewarded, they can become self-managing. Self-managed teams are not teams without leaders, but teams that are given a high degree of autonomy – they are given the power to make decisions with very limited supervision from managers as to how they use that power. They are still accountable for what they do, but the way they are accountable is based on a few specific, agreed outcomes. The organisation allows teams the freedom to make a wide range of decisions and to communicate with customers, suppliers and other teams, without managers controlling what they say or how they say it.

In return, the team is expected to perform very well. This may be measured by the level of output or the money earned. The team members may, for example, be expected to achieve a certain level of quality in what they produce or even to ensure that the level of quality is continuously improved. They may be expected to use resources efficiently and to reduce costs over time. The example of Semco (opposite) shows how one organisation has taken autonomy as far as it can.

## The Semco story

Semco is a Brazilian company owned by a family called Semler. When Ricardo Semler took over the running of the company it was managed very traditionally. In Brazil this meant that the managers were dictatorial and there were constant battles with the trades unions. At first Ricardo carried on in the same way but after a serious heart attack he decided to change the business radically, as he explained in his best-selling book, *Maverick*.

One effect of his changes was that the teams responsible for a particular activity were encouraged to take on more and more responsibility to the point where they were allowed to set up their own businesses. Semco then rented them space and equipment, gave them contracts to supply parts and encouraged them to look for additional customers. This helped Semco and the new businesses to cope better with the uncertainties of the Brazilian economy.

## Letting go

Not many self-managing teams go as far as Semco, but they can be much like mini-businesses that operate on their own account and are answerable to the organisation that employs them. Very few teams become fully self-managing, although a lot are moving towards it. It is often the last few steps that are the hardest, not just for the team but also for the organisation that has to let go of the control.

The most important factor needed for this 'letting go' to happen is *trust*. The organisation must trust the team to make full use of the autonomy that comes with self-management.

You can build trust in your team and your leadership by being:

- consistent – in how you work towards achieving the team goals

- reliable – by doing what you say you will do

- honest – by, for instance, openly acknowledging that you have made a mistake.

Trust can take a long time to build, and it can be lost in an instant because of one mistake. Think of it as a greasy pole. As your team moves farther up the pole towards the top (being self-managing), the pole gets greasier. The higher you get, the easier it is to slip back, and once you start slipping it's hard to stop.

### Team leading

As team leader you are in a position to involve team members in decision-making, encouraging them to share responsibility and be accountable for their actions. In the process they have to appreciate the importance of trust and not to abuse the opportunity to be involved in decision-making.

In return, you need to encourage your line manager to respect your team's ability to take these decisions and to allow them to take on more responsibility. Over time, with care, the team can become more autonomous and work towards being self-managing.

## Summary

- Power can be shared without being reduced. Empowering teams does not reduce the power of managers or team leaders, but adds to the power in the organisation.

- Empowerment involves delegating authority to individuals and teams based on trust, and making team members accountable for their own actions.

- Accountability involves accepting responsibility for the decisions you and the team make and the consequences of them.

- Self-managed teams are teams that have been given a degree of autonomy that allows them to make most decisions affecting their work in return for clear accountability for the outcomes.

## Review your learning

Look at the criteria for sharing decisions on page 15. Think of some specific decisions that you or your team could be faced with at work.

- Which of these criteria apply to each of these specific decisions?

- Who normally makes these decisions?

- Are there opportunities to delegate more decision-making?

> By delegating responsibility to others, you give them the power to make decisions in your place. This adds to the total amount of power.

# 4 | Building teams

## Introduction

It is all very well to talk about teams having power, but to be able to use power properly team members need to be able to work together. This chapter outlines the main processes and stages that groups can go through on their way to becoming effective and self-managed teams. You will find out more about the norms that shape the behaviour of people in teams, how these norms are decided, the effects they can have and what this means for the team's members, leaders and employers.

## How teams are formed

To understand how work *teams* are formed, it is first worth considering work *groups*, which can be seen as the first steps in building a team. An effective work group is likely to have:

- a leader who has a clear focus on making the best use of individual group members' abilities
- clearly defined roles and responsibilities (telling group members what their job is) and accountability for achieving individual goals
- no distinctive purpose, other than to work towards whatever the organisation is aiming for
- little opportunity to discuss problems or tasks (once decisions are made by their leader or manager they each get on with their own tasks).

The distinctive features of a work group in comparison to a work team are:

- an emphasis on individuals, not the group
- a sense of being just a part of a larger organisation, not a sense of being a part of a particular team
- a leader's role that is to control activity and ensure that things are done by individuals, rather than a leader's role that is just one part of the group members' shared responsibility.

Employers use work groups like this for ease of control, because they assume that without some form of supervision not much work would get done. The tasks the group performs are likely to be routine ones, so there isn't much chance to vary what individuals do, let alone how they do it. Managers also assume that if the group members were given any power to make decisions, their own power would be weakened. This attitude results from managers' views about what makes people work hard, or not – a view that was labelled 'Theory X' management by the American academic Douglas McGregor.

## Theory X

'Theory X' managers think people are reluctant to work, do not enjoy work and need supervision to make sure that they do work. In the worst cases, they assume employees are out to get as much money as they can for as little work as possible. The Theory X attitude was summed up by one team member in a plastics factory who said that before team working was introduced, managers expected him to 'leave his brain in a box by the door'.

## Theory Y

But not all managers think this way. Many managers think that the people they employ want to do their work well and are keen to have a say in what they do and how they do it. McGregor called this attitude 'Theory Y' management. Team working is based on 'Theory Y'. When team working was introduced into the plastics factory another worker said, 'I enjoy coming to work now. I like to think of ways that we can do our jobs better and know that I am valued for what I can bring to the job.'

# Getting started with work groups

Teams will be able to develop only if managers are willing to let them. Managers need to see a benefit from team working and believe that team working is possible. In other words, they must have the 'Theory Y' approach.

Managers need to create the conditions for team working by showing respect for the people in the work groups, giving them responsibility for their work and the freedom to decide how to do it. The group's members also need to feel part of the group, which often shows itself when group members start talking about the group as 'us', start to feel pride in the group or, when things go wrong, defend other group members.

The sense of belonging to an identifiable group is important because a group or team does not exist in the same way that a lump of stone exists. You can't see the group or touch it, only the people who are in it. However, once the group sees itself as a group it is starting out on the road to being a team.

The first formal studies of work groups and teams were done at the beginning of the twentieth century, but it was not until after 1945 that there was a real change in managers' thinking. There were two reasons for this. The first was research that suggested it was easier to change the way that groups thought and behaved than it was to change individuals. The second was the impact of Japanese manufacturing practices. Let's look at each of these in turn.

## Groups encourage change

Organisations that wanted to introduce new ways of working or use new technology found that working with groups was more effective than working with individuals. This is because groups tend to reinforce changes in behaviour. As the group develops its own identity, the members' different way of working becomes part of what identifies them. Reinforcement means that when something successful happens it makes it more certain that it will happen again in the future. When one person does something that the group accepts, other group members are more likely to copy it, making it more certain that the group will do it in future.

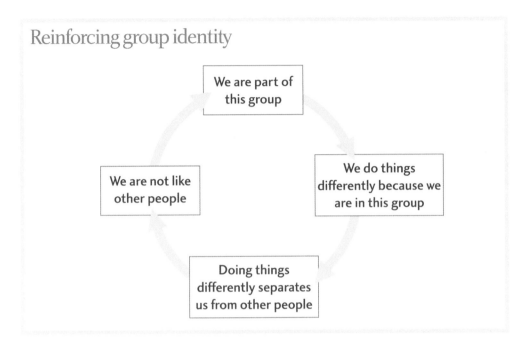

Reinforcing group identity

We are part of this group

We do things differently because we are in this group

Doing things differently separates us from other people

We are not like other people

## Japanese quality circles and teams

In the 1960s Japanese manufacturers like Toyota, Honda, Suzuki, Sony and Panasonic had an enormous impact, pushing out well-established companies in Europe and North America. The cornerstone of their success was quality and value for customers. They achieved this by using quality circles and quality improvement teams in which groups of people involved in production work together to solve quality problems and reduce costs.

Many of these ideas are now mainstream in the UK. Even so, unless work groups are allowed the freedom to make decisions and are respected for their superior knowledge about the things that they do in their jobs, then quality improvement rarely happens. In other words, work groups have to start becoming work *teams*.

## How groups become teams

Once people start to recognise that they are part of a group, they have taken the first step to becoming a team. But just taking this first step isn't a guarantee that they will eventually become a team.

A group of people with more or less the same skills will always be limited in how far they can progress because a really effective team requires people with different skills who work together and are dependent on one another.

## Skills

Groups of people who do not have adequate skills to complete their tasks well will not form effective teams. They will also need a *range* of skills, so that people can help or replace one another as needed. The team members also require team-skills, such as coaching or training other people, creating good personal relationships, being good at coming up with new ideas and, of course, being able to *lead* the team. It's important to remember that team-skills are just as important for teams as their task-skills.

## Interdependence

With this range of skills and responsibilities comes interdependence, so that the team's members rely on one another to do their jobs well. This reliance may mean rallying round when someone is off sick or under pressure to get a job finished, or passing on skills through training or coaching. The willingness of the team's members to be interdependent grows from the trust and the respect that the team members have for one another.

## Trust

Trust is based on being open, doing what you say you are going to do, and not promising what you cannot deliver. You need to be consistent, reliable and honest. It takes a long time to build trust, but losing trust takes no time at all. Too often we make promises that we cannot keep out of a mistaken belief that it will please people. Unfortunately, when we don't deliver, we really disappoint them. It's better to tell the truth and to do what you said you'd do, than to raise false hopes. Someone who keeps making mistakes, or cuts corners, or doesn't care about the job is unlikely to inspire trust. Knowing that someone has consistently done a good job means that you will trust them to keep doing a good job.

## Respect

Respect and trust are often linked. The word 'respect' can mean that you admire someone, and it can also mean that you are prepared to acknowledge someone's views and be considerate. Respect enables you to listen to someone's opinion and consider it, even if your own views are very different. Respect enables you to accept feedback about how well you perform. Accepting feedback from others helps you to learn and to improve your performance.

Teams are built on mutual respect, allowing members to contribute their ideas and to criticise one another, without being hurt or becoming defensive. Work *groups* that can encourage and accept criticism are well on the way to becoming *teams*. At times, respect may involve team members in acknowledging differences, but agreeing to a way forward.

Respect is particularly important as workplaces become more diverse and organisations work towards inclusivity. 'Diversity' means that colleagues come from different backgrounds, have physical differences and different attitudes and values. 'Inclusivity' involves ensuring that individuals or groups of people are not excluded

> Teams are built on mutual respect, allowing members to contribute their ideas and to criticise one another, without being hurt or becoming defensive.

from the workplace, decision-making, opportunities, recognition or benefits. Teams cannot be built on prejudice, a failure to respect other people's attitudes and beliefs, or exclusion. We will return to this in Chapter 16.

## Forming, storming, norming, performing

One of the most influential ideas about how work groups form into an effective unit was developed by American academic Bruce Tuckman. He suggested that all groups go through four stages that he called 'forming, storming, norming and performing'.

### Forming

At first the group doesn't have any direction and depends upon the leader of the group to give it structure and purpose. It is really just a number of individuals who happen to be working together.

### Storming

The next stage is when people start building relationships with each other. Some will try to dominate and push their ideas, leading to disagreements and making some people a little lost and worried, so that group leaders have to ensure a fair balance, defuse any conflict and assert their authority.

### Norming

Now the group has started to settle down. Relationships are built, the people feel part of a group, share ideas and feelings, and reach agreement. People can also start to lose sight of what they are trying to do, focussing on social activity rather than the task. The leader's job is to bring the group back on track.

### Performing

Now the group is focussed on what needs to be done. The group members share ideas, agree goals and get on with the job, making the leader's job a lot easier. However, the group can run into problems so the leader's job is very much about monitoring what is happening and ensuring that problems are dealt with quickly and effectively.

## Using Tuckman's model

Tuckman's model (forming, storming, norming, performing) is widely used in designing team-building activities. It gives a clear series of steps that groups can take as they move towards being teams. It is most useful if the team is just being formed (perhaps as a project team, working group or quality circle), or is about to undertake a new process.

It is *less* useful if you have been working together for some time, as there is a gradual and continual process of team development already under way. Even so, Tuckman's model does emphasise how important it is that the group members:

- recognise that they belong to the group
- have effective working relationships based on agreed goals
- understand one another and are prepared to share ideas and feelings.

## From groups to teams

In the 1990s, the Rover Car Company was keen to encourage team working and carried out a detailed study of the development stages that groups went through to become self-managing teams. They identified ten steps in the process (outlined in the box below), from first being formed into groups, to being self-managing.

---

### Rover's ten stages of team formation

Step 1    **Groups are formed, with a team leader and a structure.**

Step 2    **Group members have their own development plans (to raise skills levels) and have clear team roles.**

Step 3    **Teams develop their own rules and start to take responsibility for their own tools and equipment.**

Step 4    **Teams start to liaise with customers and suppliers, and have further responsibility for their tools and equipment.**

Step 5    **Teams start to plan their work and have full responsibility for their tools and equipment.**

Step 6    **Teams are working with customers and suppliers, and reviewing their own performance, to improve processes.**

Step 7    **Teams are able to handle internal conflicts and appraise their manager.**

Step 8    **Teams set their own targets and plan and control costs.**

Step 9    **Teams are fully skilled and recruit and induct new members.**

Step 10   **Teams are self-managed.**

---

Some of these steps are similar to Tuckman's stages, but are part of a more detailed and structured process. Tuckman was looking at groups of people who were already skilled and were coming together for a *project*. The ten Rover stages reflect the need for people in teams to develop and widen their skills – which takes time. Rover also included the need for effective working relationships and for agreement on goals, which depend on trust and mutual respect. The company also:

- invested heavily in training, to enable people to develop the skills they needed

- made a clear place for teams in the organisation

- ensured that the team tasks were suitable for team working.

This support for both individuals and for teams was crucial. Without it, each team would have been just another work *group*, not a real *team*.

## Suitability

Not every job or person is suitable for team working. Teams should not be expected to work where they don't have a role. People who prefer to work on their own shouldn't be forced into a team role. For instance, those who visit clients to repair equipment, and are happier with machines than with other people, are better off being allowed to work as individuals, not as members of teams. Use teams where they offer benefits, and include people in teams where they and the team will benefit, but don't assume that it is *always* the best way to work.

## Summary

- Developing teams involves a switch of emphasis from *individual* members of a work group to the *group as a whole*.

- The 'Theory Y' management style, which assumes that people want to work well and are motivated to achieve a high performance, encourages the move to team working.

- People have to feel part of a distinct group, to have an identity, before they can start to become a team.

- If they are to make the change from a group to a team, the members of groups need to develop their range of skills, become more interdependent, and trust and respect one another.

## Review your learning

Look at your work group or team. What stage has it reached in its development from a group to a team? In particular, ask yourself the following questions.

- Do members have a range of skills or do they mainly perform separate tasks relying on different skills?

- How interdependent are they? Do they work together, relying on one another's contribution to overall output?

- How much trust is there in the team? Do people assume that if someone says they will do something, it will be done, and will be done well?

- Do the members show respect for one another, both in their task-related knowledge and skills, and in their team-related skills?

# 5 | Working towards goals

## Introduction

Teams are groups of people with different skills working together in an organised way to achieve their goals. Goals give team members a shared focus and sense of direction, in the same way that players in games like football, rugby, hockey, hurling and lacrosse all aim to score goals. Their shared purpose is the goal, whether it is the back of the net, a production schedule, or customer approval.

In this chapter you'll find out how goals identify and describe a team's purpose and can help teams to function well. You will also find out about SMART goals, how goals are agreed and what happens if they are not agreed.

## What are goals?

Imagine you are setting out on a journey. You might be like Christopher Columbus, with just a direction to go in ('head west'), or like modern travellers, with a specific destination. If you have really planned your journey well, you may also have a few milestones on the way to help you to confirm that you are on the right road. Each of these aspects of your journey (direction, destination and milestones) could be thought of as different types of goal.

## Direction

One feature of direction is that you can never arrive. You can keep heading west for the rest of your life and still not arrive at the place called 'west'. That does not stop it from being a very definite direction and one that can keep you going straight (or, to be precise, in a circle around the globe). If you deviate from due west, you will lose your direction and finish up in places you didn't intend to visit.

## Destination

A destination is much clearer. If you were setting out to go west from London, Cardiff, Edinburgh, Belfast or Dublin, then your destination might be Bristol, Swansea, Glasgow, Omagh or Athlone, respectively. A destination is very different from a direction. You can arrive at a destination and know that you have arrived.

## Milestones

Milestones are places you must pass through on your way to your destination. They help you to measure your progress and they divide a journey up into less daunting chunks. They may just be a service station or junction on the motorway, but they provide a waymarker for the journey to tell you that you are on the right route and have travelled a certain distance.

# Goals at work

What has this got to do with goals at *work*? In practice, we tend to come across all three different types of goal – direction goals, destination goals and milestone goals. As you will see, they serve the same functions as their travelling counterparts.

## Mission statements give direction

Direction goals are designed to give an organisation, a division of an organisation or a team a sense of purpose. They say 'this is the way we are heading'. The most common type of direction goal is the mission statement. The best mission statements give everyone in the organisation, its suppliers and customers a real sense of where the organisation is heading. Mission statements are sometimes called an organisation's 'aims', because they say where the organisation wants to go. They may also be linked to its values – what the organisation considers to be important.

You will see from the examples of mission statements below how difficult it would be to measure how well the goals are being achieved. However, you can make a judgement about whether or not the organisations are still heading in the right direction by setting a destination that is in that direction.

---

## Mission statements

Marks and Spencer **"to make aspirational quality accessible to all"**

Epilepsy Scotland **"working to overcome ignorance and injustice faced by people with epilepsy throughout Scotland"**

University of Cambridge **"to contribute to society through the pursuit of education, learning, and research at the highest international levels of excellence"**

Barloworld **"to be the customers' first choice in providing cost-effective materials-handling solutions"**

BT **"to be the best provider of communications services and solutions for everybody in the UK and for corporate customers in the rest of Europe, with global reach through partnerships"**

---

## Objectives set destinations

Objectives are the organisation's destination, the *specific* outcomes that the organisation expects to achieve. Unlike a mission statement or aims, an objective should be achievable, just like reaching a destination, and the people who work for the organisation should be able to judge when the objective has been achieved.

An organisation's objectives are often expressed in terms of money, particularly a level of turnover or revenue (how much the organisation earns). The objectives can also be for a particular level of growth in turnover or customers, or a percentage reduction in costs or faulty goods returned, a particular market share (proportion of the total market for a product or service) or level of customer satisfaction.

In larger organisations the various divisions may set objectives that are designed to help to achieve the whole organisation's objectives. In turn, teams may have objectives designed to help the division to achieve its objectives. In this way, if every team reaches its objectives, then the division hits its objectives. If every division hits its objectives, then the organisation does so too. That's the theory, at least.

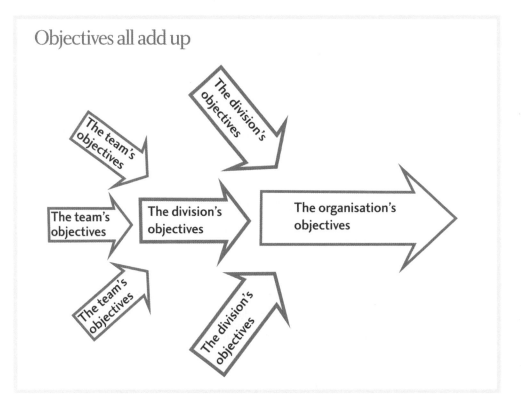

## Objectives all add up

The team's objectives

The division's objectives

The team's objectives

The division's objectives

The team's objectives

The division's objectives

The organisation's objectives

## Milestones measure progress

Milestones tell you how far you've travelled and that you are on the right road. Milestones are sometimes called targets, because they are short-term objectives. Don't worry about the label, just be aware that they are not where you are headed, but markers on the way. Organisations often break their objectives into quarterly, monthly or even weekly targets. These can be simply a $1/4$, $1/12$ or $1/52$ of the annual objective, but they may reflect different patterns of activity across the year. For example, an ice cream company in the UK may have turnover targets for the three summer months that are greater than for the other nine. Department stores in the

UK expect to sell far more in the three months leading up to Christmas than they do in each of the other three quarters of the year. If your organisation sets milestones like this, you should find out whether they show similar patterns.

## Teams have goals

Without goals, teams will really only be work groups. Goals give the team a sense of shared purpose, for which the individual members have responsibility. That's why teams can have their own mission statements, objectives and milestones, each designed to give them this clear purpose.

### A team with a mission

It may not be necessary for a team to have its own mission statement, but it can help to give the team a clear identity and help the team's members to recognise what they are trying to achieve collectively. The statement may be something like:

- to delight our customers (*in a customer service centre*)
- to respond quickly, courteously and cleanly (*repairing burst water mains*)
- supplying quality, when it is wanted, where it is wanted (*a production team*).

It may be hard to measure the achievement of these goals, but they certainly give a team a sense of direction.

### Team objectives

Teams don't need to have a mission but they do need to have objectives. Without them the team is aimless, just a group of people working together. The team's objectives should say what the team has to achieve, when the objectives have to be achieved by and how the team will know whether or not the objectives have been achieved. The best way to judge if objectives do this is to ask whether they are SMART, which stands for:

- **S**pecific
- **M**easurable
- **A**greed (or **a**chievable)
- **R**ealistic (or **r**esourced)
- **T**imed.

If the objectives are specific, then you know precisely what they are. Saying, "We will improve quality" is not specific. Saying, "We will reduce rejects to 0.4%" is specific. It's also measurable, so you will know whether or not you have achieved it.

Objectives must also be agreed, by the team and by your manager. The team is responsible for achieving the objectives so the team members need to agree them (or they will not try to achieve them). As the team is accountable to your manager, your manager also needs to have agreed them. But it's no use agreeing objectives if

Goals give the team a sense of shared purpose, for which the individual members have responsibility.

they cannot be achieved, so they have to be realistic. You also need to know *when* they are they supposed to be achieved, or else how will you know when to measure them? That's why they need to have a time limit. Here are some examples of SMART team objectives:

- to reduce customer waiting times to less than three minutes by the end of this quarter
- to arrive at all emergencies within three hours of being called
- to reduce reject rates to 0.4% over the whole year.

(In the alternative version of SMART, the A is for *achievable*, which is more or less the same as realistic. The R in this version is for *resourced*, indicating that objectives will be resourced only if they are agreed.)

## Milestones for teams

Milestones are often used by project teams to help them to break the whole project into bite-sized chunks. But all teams can use them to help them to achieve their objectives. Milestones help you to reduce daunting objectives to something that everyone feels comfortable with. If, for example, the team is trying to get customer waiting times down to three minutes and is currently keeping 20 per cent of customers waiting for five minutes, then milestones may be:

- no customer kept waiting for more than four minutes
- 90% of customers responded to within three minutes.

These two milestones help the team to measure its progress towards its objectives. Once these short-term objectives are achieved, then the team can move closer to the final objective.

## Stretch goals

One of the big advantages of goals is that they motivate people. There's more about this in Chapter 14, but it is something to think about when setting team goals. 'To motivate' means that people are enthusiastic, committed and willing to work as well as they are able. Goals can help to motivate people because the sense of accomplishment that comes from achieving goals encourages people to reach them.

However, goals that are too easy to reach have less motivational effect. Goals that are too hard have no effect at all because people know they will not achieve them. The best goals are *demanding* but *achievable*, and are known as stretch goals. They encourage people to put in just that little bit extra without being so demanding that people are disheartened by them.

If the team members are involved in agreeing objectives, then they will want goals that are not going to be too hard. Your task, as team leader, is to encourage them to think about doing that little bit extra and to agree to objectives that stretch them without breaking them. Only you can judge what is going to stretch them and what is likely to take them to breaking point. It is far better to get the team members to add a little bit to their objectives at regular intervals, so that they get a little bit better every time, than to expect them to increase performance dramatically in one go.

Individual team members should have goals that help them to achieve the team's goals, in just the same way that the team's goals contribute to the division's or organisation's goals. However, it is important that individual goals are seen as contributing to, and not replacing, team goals. In a real team it is the team's goals that matter. The individuals channel the team's energies and attention into what the team has to achieve collectively, and what the team is accountable for.

> In a real team it is the team's goals that matter.

## Summary

- Organisations can have three types of goal. Their direction is in the mission statement, their destination is in their objectives and their milestones are in their short-term objectives or targets.

- Teams need to have objectives. These give the team members their collective purpose, focus their energies, motivate them and make clear what they are accountable for.

- The best objectives are SMART (specific, measurable, agreed, realistic and timed). There are also stretch goals, encouraging just that little bit extra.

- Individual goals should be based on the team's goals and help to achieve, not replace, them.

## Review your learning

Look at your team's objectives and compare them to the SMART criteria.

- Are they SMART? If not, what needs to be done to them to make them SMART?

- Are there stretch goals? Do they ask for extra effort without being unattainable?

- If the goals are not stretch goals, what would be better stretch goals for your team?

# The effective team leader

Leadership has become a popular discussion topic. Organisations are looking for more than effective management (although they still need that). They also want leadership – to provide vision and a sense of direction. But leadership does not exist only at the top of organisations. Leadership is needed all the way through an organisation. Most importantly, it is needed at the point where things happen, in the teams that produce the goods and services for the organisation.

This section looks at leadership – what it is, how you can develop yourself to become an effective team leader and, in particular, the importance of communication as a leadership skill and activity.

There are many theories of leadership and it used to be thought that you were either a leader or you were not. But it is now widely agreed that most people are capable of developing the skills needed to be effective in the role. This section will help you to do so.

The first step is to understand what a team leader does, what the role involves and which skills it calls for. It is also important to realise that some ways of leading people are more effective than others at particular times and in specific circumstances. An awareness of likely appropriate behaviour at any particular time will help you to gain confidence in yourself and in your ability to lead other people. Team leaders need to inspire confidence in others. You can help to achieve this by feeling in control of yourself and your work, and being able to communicate well with your team, your managers and others.

# 6 | What is leadership?

## Introduction

Now it is time to focus on *leading* the team and the role of the team leader. So far we have concentrated on what teams are, how they work, how they are formed and their goals. Leadership is central to all these. In this chapter you will read about some of the main ideas about leadership. There are many of them, and although they may at first look quite different, they tend to share some clear similarities. The first part of this chapter looks at what some of these ideas can tell us about leadership. We then look at how leadership is related to power and how effective leaders are able to motivate people to do things.

## Leadership

Leadership abilities include persuading, influencing or inspiring others to achieve a particular goal. This is different from *making* people do something. An effective leader is able to motivate people to achieve goals because they want to achieve them. The key question is how? How do leaders create the willingness among other people to be followers? Answers to this question can be found in some of the most significant theories about leadership – the 'great man', trait and behaviour theories.

## The 'great man' theory of leadership

One of the early approaches to explaining leadership is called the 'great man' theory. It assumes that men like Winston Churchill, Mahatma Ghandi and Nelson Mandela, who all played critical roles in helping their countries through difficult times, were able to be great leaders because of who they were – that it was something about their background and upbringing that made them the leaders they became.

### A 'great' leader?

Winston Churchill is widely regarded as one of the most significant leaders of the twentieth century. He could be very emotional and sometimes interfered and bullied people. But he also stood firm to his beliefs, trusted people who showed they could deliver and respected those who stood up to him. Perhaps his most important personal qualities were his willingness to work hard, to travel widely to meet people and, above all, to communicate. He prepared his own speeches and chose his words carefully, so as to be honest (even when things were going badly) but at the same time to inspire people to believe that things would improve.

At one time it was thought that some people (a minority) were born to be leaders and the rest (the majority) were born to be the people they led. It is clearer now that past leaders did not just inherit their ability to be leaders, but, among other things, they were confident that they could be leaders. Confidence is an important feature of successful leaders: you can encourage other people to believe in you if you believe in yourself. (You can become more confident by developing the leadership skills described later in the book.)

### Charisma

Perhaps a better description of many of the greatest leaders is that they had charisma. Charisma is the inbuilt ability that some people seem to have to inspire others. You probably know one or two people like that, who always seem to make a party go better when they are there, who are good to have in meetings because they make everyone feel that they will achieve something. Charismatic figures are few and far between, and we can't all be like that.

Perhaps there are occasions when we need charismatic people, but charisma doesn't explain why some people make great leaders. In fact some charismatic leaders, such as Hitler and Stalin, are widely viewed today, as they were by many at the time, as evil people, so it is difficult to argue that they were 'great men'.

### Great women

It is also worth noting that the term 'great men' is misleading, as it suggests that leaders cannot be female. What, for example, about Boudicca, Queen Elizabeth I, Golda Meir, Indira Ghandi or Emmeline Pankhurst? They were not 'great men', but they are acknowledged as very effective leaders.

### Complexity

The more we look at great historical leaders it becomes clear that they were all very different, which suggests that leadership is more complex than simply fitting into a single mould labelled 'great men'. This is why studies of leadership have looked in more detail at what it really is that makes people leaders.

## The trait theory of leadership

Perhaps a better explanation of people who are considered to be effective leaders is that they have a certain personality trait or a collection of traits.

Personality is what makes you the person you are – the mixture of characteristics like intelligence, your ability and willingness to be outgoing, your ability to relate to other people, your forcefulness and your conscientiousness. You'll find a list (opposite) of the 23 traits that the United States army considers to be important for leadership.

Trait theory suggests that leadership depends largely on being born with the particular personality traits needed to be a leader, or developing those traits as a child. According to this theory, some people have these traits and others do not, and there is not very much that either group can do about it.

Looking at people who seem to be good leaders it is clear that there are some types of personality that probably *prevent* people from being good leaders. People who are very introverted (inward-looking people) are unlikely to be effective leaders. People who are unimaginative or not very bright are unlikely to inspire people to follow them. People who are very dogmatic (who won't listen to others' points of view), argumentative or dictatorial may be able to *drive* people but are unlikely to be able to lead them.

In contrast, extroverted (outgoing), imaginative, open-minded people who listen are more likely to be able to influence others to follow them. This suggests that there is something useful in trait theory, but it may not give the whole picture.

## The American army's traits of character

The US Army has identified 23 traits that it regards as important for effective leadership.

- Bearing
- Confidence
- Courage
- Integrity
- Decisiveness
- Justice
- Endurance
- Tact
- Initiative
- Coolness
- Maturity
- Improvement
- Will
- Assertiveness
- Candour
- Sense of humour
- Competence
- Commitment
- Creativity
- Self-discipline
- Humility
- Flexibility
- Empathy/compassion

Leadership abilities include persuading, influencing or inspiring others to achieve a particular goal. This is different from *making* people do something.

# Behaviour theories of leadership

Behaviour theories suggest that people can *learn* how to be leaders by developing many of the *skills* that are needed by effective leaders. People with the 'wrong kind' of personality traits would probably have difficulty in learning these behaviours, but they might still be able to do so.

## Inspiring others

The American leadership gurus Warren Bennis and Burt Nanus describe leaders as 'pulling rather than pushing'. They say that leaders *inspire* people to follow their lead (and achieve challenging goals or meet high expectations), rather than having to *order* them to do things. Leaders do this by rewarding progress (not with money, but with praise and support) and by encouraging people to use their own initiative and draw on their own experience as they work towards the goals. Bennis and Nanus suggest that there are four main groups of behaviour (which they call 'strategies' – see the box below) that enable leaders to inspire others.

---

## Four strategies for leadership

Attention through vision: **keeping your attention focussed all the time on what you are trying to achieve – your goals.**

Meaning through communication: **using your communication skills to influence your team members so that they share the same goals.**

Trust through positioning: **clearly, consistently and reliably communicating what you mean and sticking to it.**

Deployment of self: **having a strong sense of your own worth and skills, and continuing to try to improve yourself and your performance.**

---

Most of us can learn and develop these four 'strategies'. They basically involve:

- being goal-focussed
- communicating well
- being trustworthy
- valuing yourself while striving to improve.

The Harvard Business School professor John Kotter emphasises three broadly similar sets of behaviour:

- establishing direction – having both a vision of the future and ways to achieve it
- aligning people – being able to communicate the direction to everyone you need to take with you
- motivating and inspiring – actively involving people in making things happen.

Kotter has another version of 'pushing and pulling', which he describes as 'positional power' and 'personal power'. Positional power is the power that comes from the job position you hold – "I am the team leader, you must do what I say." Positional power means that you reward people for doing what you want, and punish those who do not. However, Kotter says that effective leaders achieve far more by using their personal power. This means that others believe in you and trust you to make the right decisions. Alternatively, they admire you, or think you are the obvious choice to make decisions because you have specific knowledge.

### Transactional and transformational leaders

Another popular model of leadership (by James MacGregor Burns) describes two different ways of leading people. The first, which he calls transactional leadership, is where followers do what they are asked (or told to do) because of the leaders' promises, rewards or threats of disciplinary action. But leaders can ask people to do only what they are *contracted* to do, which is why it is a transaction. The alternative form, transformational leadership, is based on leaders being able to inspire others by their high standards, challenging people to help to achieve shared goals, encouraging people to be innovative and, all the time, treating each person as an individual. One significant feature of transformational leadership is the high moral or ethical standards that leaders show. Burns believed that the most effective leaders were people who showed, by their high standards, the sort of behaviour that other people would value and try to copy.

## Becoming a leader

So what should you do? Is leadership all about personality traits, or is it about your behaviour? Do you need to be goal-focussed and trustworthy, communicate well, and value yourself while striving to improve? Do you need to use your personal power or be a transformational leader?

## From theory to the workplace

Most of these theories have some value, but may not be the whole truth. In practice, effective leaders behave in certain ways and they are likely to have certain personality traits that make it more likely that they will behave in such ways. Even so, many of the theories outlined in this chapter overlap, and it is possible to draw these traits and behaviour together into a single list (see box on page 38). You may find it helpful to consider which of these reflect you and your leadership style, and which, if you developed them, could help you to become a more effective leader.

However, you should not go away with the idea that you have to be good at *all* of the points on the list to be effective. Rather, these are what effective leaders *tend* to be good at, but not necessarily all leaders are good at all of them. What you need to do is to work out which ones you are good at and how you can develop those that need improving. The rest of *Leading Teams* can help you to do so.

## The most important characteristics of leaders

1. Communication and social skills.

2. Personal drive, sense of purpose and motivation.

3. Dependability, conscientiousness and persistence.

4. Ability to motivate others.

5. Innovation and vision.

6. Honesty and integrity.

7 Self-confidence, willingness to accept challenges and take risks, emotional maturity.

8. Ability to inspire trust.

9. Intelligence.

10. Knowledge about the organisation you work for.

11. Genuine interest in others and valuing them.

12. A team orientation (you like working with a team of people).

## Summary

- Most ideas about leadership fall into three broad categories, the 'great man' theories, trait theories and behaviour theories.

- 'Great man' theories see leaders as a small minority, and tend to emphasise background, upbringing and charisma.

- Trait theories focus on personality and suggest that leaders are people who are outgoing, imaginative, open-minded and prepared to listen to others.

- Behaviour theories emphasise the skills that leaders have; skills that can be learnt by most people, to a greater or lesser extent. These skills include being goal-focussed, able to communicate well with others and to motivate or inspire them, being honest, consistent, dependable and conscientious.

- Leaders are people who do not need to rely on the power of their position to get people to do things ('push'), but can use their personal power (who they are, how they behave) to get people to follow them ('pull').

## Review your learning

Think about the people you know who you regard as effective leaders. They can be public figures (politicians or business leaders, for example) and people you know personally.

- What is it about them that makes you think of them as effective leaders?

- How do you rate them on each of the 12 characteristics listed in the box above?

# 7 | Becoming a team leader

## Introduction

What do team leaders do? What are their roles, responsibilities, authority and accountability? And what is *outside* their remit? This chapter looks at the role of the team leader with regard to the team, the task and the individual team member. It links closely to Chapter 8, which suggests different ways in which team leaders can carry out their roles.

## The role of the team leader

Managers generally do different tasks from the people they manage, or they do the same tasks for only a part of the time. Team leaders are not managers. They spend most of their time doing what their team does. They are usually part of the team, working alongside other team members and doing more or less the same sort of tasks as the others, but with additional responsibilities.

The difference between team leaders and managers is important. If team leaders cannot do what the team members can do, then their authority is likely to be weakened. This is why most team leaders are appointed only if they are at least as good at their tasks as everyone else in the team.

### Control

As we have also seen, teams should, ideally, not have more than about a dozen people, so the team leader's span of control – the number of people for whom the team leader is responsible – is quite small. If there are many people, it is hard for the team leader to know each member well, know what each is capable of doing or even what they are doing.

### Day-to-day responsibility

Team leaders tend to focus on the short term, on the day-to-day performance of the team and its members. They tend to be responsible for allocating each day's tasks between team members (or making sure that tasks are allocated). This is why they need to know what each person is capable of doing. They are also responsible for ensuring that output meets the requirements of the organisation and its customers, both in terms of quantity (the right amount of work being done or goods produced) and quality (it is being done or produced well enough).

### Communication

Communication is a significant part of a team leader's role. Team leaders act as the bridge between the management of the organisation and the team, and this bridge should have a two-way flow. As a consequence, team leaders need to know what they are allowed to do and what falls to their managers to decide. They also need to know what they need to tell their managers about and what they do not need to report.

## Action-centred leadership

It's helpful to consider the team leader's role under the headings of 'team', 'task' and 'the individual'. The headings come from the 'action-centred leadership' model created by John Adair, a leading British leadership pioneer. As the name implies, the model deals with what team leaders actually do – their actions. Often described as Adair's 'three-circle model', the model uses three interlocking circles to illustrate how the main areas of a team leader's responsibilities fit together.

1. Achieving the task (making sure that the team achieves its goals, that team members do what they should be doing).

2. Maintaining the team (ensuring that the team members work together effectively as a team).

3. Developing the individual (making sure that people have the knowledge and skills they need, and taking action if they don't).

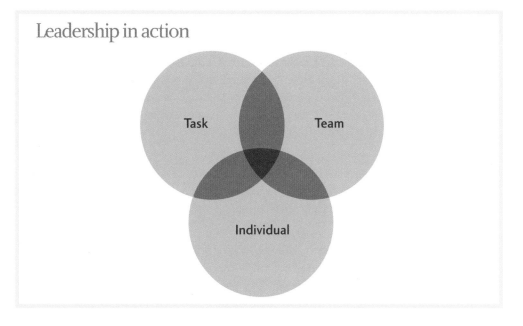

Leadership in action

Task    Team

Individual

## Using the three-circle model

Most of the things a team leader does involve more than one aspect of the role. A production difficulty, for example, may be due to a problem with materials (task-related). However, the person affected did not think to mention it to you (the individual) and nobody else in the team took any notice (team). The model can help you to identify whether an aspect of your role is:

- a *task* problem (unclear goals or responsibilities, lack of materials, faulty equipment, for example)

- a *team* problem (tensions in the team, poor communication between team members, for example)

- an *individual* problem (lack of skills, lack of motivation, personal problems at home, for example).

You can use the model to think about the skills that team leaders need. When facing a specific situation you can ask yourself which aspect – the task, the team or the individual – is particularly relevant.

# The power and authority of a team leader

In Chapter 6 different approaches to leadership described leaders as 'pulling rather than pushing'; as using 'personal', not 'positional', power; or achieving 'transformational' relationships. What all three ideas have in common is that leaders *encourage* people to do things through their *own* personality and behaviour, rather than because of the power or authority of their *role*.

This is true of all leaders, and especially team leaders. It is rare for team leaders to have much power or authority, because they are not expected to need it. Power and authority in organisations tend to include the responsibilities for:

- employing, disciplining or dismissing people

- deciding on spending or receiving money, including agreeing prices with suppliers and with customers

- deciding on what the organisation should do, such as whether to develop new products or services or to adopt new ways of working.

> Leaders *encourage* people to do things through their *own* personality and behaviour, rather than because of the power or authority of their *role*.

## What team leaders usually cannot do

In general, team leaders do not employ people (although they may be consulted when new team members are recruited). They cannot formally discipline people (although they may report them for undisciplined behaviour), and they cannot dismiss them. The only money they can spend is either from petty cash, or is subject to strict rules and controls (such as how much they can claim for an overnight stay). They might be able to offer discounts to customers, but again, these are subject to rules, such as the quantity being bought.

Team leaders cannot change the goods and services they produce or, broadly speaking, how they produce them, although they might be expected to make improvements to both as long as no major changes or any costs are involved.

## What team leaders must do

Even so, team leaders *are* expected to achieve a great deal, such as ensuring that:

- people do the jobs they are employed to do as well as they are able

- money is earned by supplying goods and services to customers, as required; materials and services are used efficiently; and money is spent safely and securely

- goods and services are supplied to the quality required, at the time and place they are required, and that opportunities are constantly sought to improve them and the way they are produced.

In other words, team leaders are accountable for an awful lot without having very much power and authority. That's why they need to pull people along (not push them) by using their personal power (not their positional power).

# The responsibilities of the team leader

John Adair's three-circle model provides a useful way of identifying and considering the responsibilities that team leaders normally have. We look at the team, task and individual in turn. However, it is important to remember that each of these responsibilities affects the other two, and all three interlink and overlap in practice, just as the three circles in the diagram overlap.

## The team

A team leader's first and foremost responsibility is to ensure that team members work effectively together as a team. Without an effective team to lead, team leaders will always find it hard to fulfil their other responsibilities. As you saw in the first five chapters, this includes:

* being aware of the benefits of team working and promoting these benefits to members of the team (or work group)

* ensuring that members of the team are aware of their roles, both their task roles (the jobs they do) and their team roles (how they help team members to perform effectively as a team)

* helping to build effective working relationships between members of the team and ensuring that the team's norms and culture do not exclude individuals

* sharing power with the team in decision-making

* helping to build the team, encouraging team members to work together, to solve problems and develop themselves

* helping new members of the team to settle in and perform effectively as quickly as possible by involving the whole team in their induction.

## The task

Later chapters deal with the tasks that teams perform and the team leader's role in making sure that these are performed to the right standard. In brief, team leaders have responsibility for ensuring that tasks are performed safely, effectively and efficiently.

### Safely
The health and safety of team members, customers and others with whom the team has contact is a major responsibility. The environment must also be protected.

### Effectively
People are increasingly demanding, and expect that they will be able to enjoy goods and services that meet their expectations in full. Quality starts in the initial design of goods and services, continues through the way that they are produced or

supplied and ends with the after-sales service that customers require. Team leaders have responsibility for the way that processes are operated, how well the goods and services meet (or exceed) the standards set, what the quality is of the service to customers and how well customers are served afterwards.

### Efficiently

All organisations, whether they are trying to make a profit (private sector organisations) or not (public and voluntary sector organisations), must use resources efficiently. Resources include machinery, vehicles, equipment, people, materials, and energy. Team leaders might have little responsibility for selecting which resources are available, but they do have responsibility for how they are used.

### Monitoring

You and your team are accountable for how safely, effectively and efficiently you perform your tasks. Many organisations monitor individuals and teams to ensure that they are being as safe, effective and efficient as they can be. One of the indicators of an organisation that is really committed to team working is that it monitors the team rather than individuals in the team. It is the team's and the team leader's responsibility to ensure that individuals meet the standards set for them.

> You and your team are accountable for how safely, effectively and efficiently you perform your tasks.

## The individual

A team is made up of individuals, and the worst thing any team leader can do is to expect everybody in the team to think and behave exactly the same. As a team leader you need to ensure that all your team members perform as well as they are able. You can do this by:

- treating people fairly
- building effective relationships
- having good communication skills
- improving team members' skills
- handling conflict.

### Treating people fairly

There is increasing legal protection for individuals to prevent discrimination at work. In the best teams, the members value people and respect one another for what they can do. In return, individuals don't deliberately attempt to provoke or annoy others by their words or behaviour. Mutual respect is the cornerstone of effective team working. As team leader it is your responsibility to demonstrate this behaviour to others, to provide a model for the rest of the team.

### Building effective relationships

You need to be good at building relationships with different people. You need to be able to understand what is important to them, so that you can motivate them to contribute as much as they can.

### Having good communication skills

You need to be able to speak to different people in ways that they will understand. More importantly, you need to be able to *listen* to them, to understand what they think and believe, so that you can build a better working relationship.

*Improving team members' skills*

You also need to be able to help your team members to improve their skills. This means being able to identify what they are good at and what they need to learn. You need to identify what is available to help them to learn and, particularly, to pass on your own skills by training and coaching team members.

*Handling conflict*

When things go wrong, you need to have the skills for handling conflict. Problems happen in the best teams, but team leaders shouldn't allow conflict between team members to fester and harm the whole team. You need to recognise the *causes* of conflict and deal with conflict when it happens. You also need to know when it has gone past the stage when *you* can do something about it, and refer it to a manager who can deal with it.

## Summary

- Team leaders are members of the team who have additional responsibilities to the rest of the team. They need to be good at doing the tasks that other team members do.

- Team leaders usually have responsibility for the task, the team and the individual, but rarely have much power and authority. They rely on their personal power if they are to ensure that the team performs to the standard required.

- Responsibility for the team includes promoting team working, ensuring that members are aware of their roles, building effective relationships, sharing power, building the team and helping new members to join the team.

- Responsibility for tasks centres on health, safety and protecting the environment, the quality of goods and services (effectiveness) and making the best use of the resources available (efficiency).

- Responsibility for individuals covers treating all people fairly, building effective relationships, good communication, helping people to improve their skills and handling conflict.

## Review your learning

Look at John Adair's action-centred leadership (three-circle) model on page 40 and the list of team leader responsibilities on pages 42 to 43.

- Which of these responsibilities are you aware of and expected to undertake?

- Which of these are responsibilities that you were *not* aware of or *not* expected to undertake?

- What do you need to do to take on any of these other responsibilities?

- In what ways could you improve your performance as a team leader by considering aspects of your role under the headings of team, task and individual?

# 8 | Developing as a leader

## Introduction

Being a leader is not something we simply choose to do, then, 'hey presto!' we are leaders. Being a leader involves understanding what kind of leadership styles you should adopt, which are the most appropriate for the specific situation, and which skills you need. Personal power comes from having skills like goal-setting, communicating, motivating and accepting challenges. You will learn more about many of these specific skills in later chapters, but this chapter focusses on how you know if you have particular skills and how to go about developing them.

## Leadership style

In Chapter 6 you read about different theories of leadership. *Leading Teams* has encouraged you to see that leadership involves you in using your knowledge and skills to behave in particular ways, and in making the most of the personality traits that can help you to behave in those ways. However, leadership is not something that involves just one particular type of behaviour. There are many possible ways to behave, and these are often referred to as leadership style. In general, leadership style tends to be a combination of how much you direct the team and how much you support team members.

### 'Directive' behaviour

*'Directive' behaviour* describes someone who is very directing; giving orders (directives), but not asking questions or listening. Such leaders have clear rules about what people should and should not do, and they tend to supervise closely. This can be useful if people are new, inexperienced or need a lot of help and clear direction. As team members become more able, however, leaders need to become more supportive.

### Supportive behaviour

*Supportive behaviour* involves asking and listening, rather than telling. It also means helping the people in the team to work together, building relationships, and encouraging people to discuss ideas with one another and to make suggestions. In particular, it means involving people in decision-making. You need to recognise the strengths and weaknesses of each leadership style, and choose the one that is right for each situation and the people involved. You may find it helpful to consider the styles as four possible extremes (see the box on page 46).

## Four leadership styles

| Style | A leader who is: |
|---|---|
| Telling | Very directing and unsupportive, focussing on the task *not* the relationship with team members. |
| Selling | Very directive but supportive, focussing on the task *and* the relationship with team members. |
| Participating | Not directing but is supportive, focussing on the relationship with team members, *not* the task. |
| Delegating | Leaders who are neither directing nor supportive, leaving the team to focus on the task *and* to support one another. |

## Combining behaviour

The four styles of telling, selling, participating and delegating are formed by linking direction and support. Team leaders need to learn which style to use, and when.

### Telling

The telling style is suitable for leaders to use with new team members who have low skill levels or experience or who need clear guidance about the task they have to perform. But there is a danger in the telling style. A leader can use it all the time and become authoritarian or dictatorial, never consulting the team or giving support to people. Teams with authoritarian leaders soon become work groups, as the people in them lose the sense of being part of a team with shared goals.

### Selling

The selling style is particularly useful when team members are more experienced but still need to develop their skills. The team leader sets the goals for the team but tries to get members to agree them. As long as the team members are willing and motivated, this style can be quite effective. (This style is sometimes described as being consultative because team leaders ask people for their views before making the decisions. However, the leaders still make the decisions themselves.)

### Participating

The participating style is very supportive and, because team members are encouraged to make decisions, is not 'directive' behaviour. It is best used when teams are skilled and able to perform tasks but perhaps still need some encouragement. The team leader's job is to encourage and help the team members (be supportive) to make decisions and carry them out.

### Delegating

The delegating style allows team members to make decisions without any involvement from the team leader. Team members are skilled and motivated and the team is well developed. Teams that have reached this stage are largely self-managing, with the team leader being largely concerned with ensuring that the team is still functioning effectively and helping new members to settle in. This leadership style can also allow team leaders to develop new skills and move their career on from the team leadership role.

## Making the style appropriate

Jacob runs a small building business. He has a small team of experienced workers who he has worked with for several years and who he trusts. He usually encourages the team to participate in decision-making and frequently delegates decision-making because he has two or three jobs on the go so cannot be around to make decisions at each site.

However, before he started his own business he worked for a larger company on big building sites. He used to lead groups of builders who had varying levels of skill and who were not very well motivated. In fact, if they could work slowly, knock off early and delay completion, it meant that they were employed for longer. As a result, he was used to being very authoritarian, telling people what to do to make sure that the job was done. One of the important things in developing himself as a leader was to recognise which leadership style was appropriate for any given situation.

## Which skills do you need?

Being a leader is largely about choosing the right behaviour. Sometimes it means doing unpleasant things because they need to be done. At other times you have to stand back and let the team members get on with something, even if you do not fully agree with what they are doing. Judging what is the right thing to do at the time is a skill you can develop only with practice, and it depends upon you having a wider set of skills. So, which skills do team leaders need? In Chapter 6 (see page 38) there was a list of the characteristics of leaders. Some of these can be translated into the specific skills, attitudes or behaviour shown in the box below.

## The skills and behaviour team leaders need

1. Communication and social skills.
2. Personal drive, sense of purpose and motivation.
3. Dependability, conscientiousness and persistence.
4. Ability to motivate others.
5. Innovation and vision.
6. Honesty and integrity.
7. Self-confidence, willingness to accept challenges and take risks, emotional maturity.
8. Ability to inspire trust.
9. Intelligence.
10. Knowledge about the organisation you work for.
11. Genuine interest in others and valuing them.
12. A team orientation (you like working with a team of people).

It is important for you, as a team leader, to take responsibility for ensuring that you have the right skills to do your job effectively. We will be looking at many of these skills or behaviours in more detail in the rest of this book.

## Living with change

The world can change fast. It took nearly a century for half the population of the UK to have a telephone after they were first being sold, but it took only about a decade for the same proportion to use mobile phones. Until the end of the nineteenth century most people rarely moved willingly more than a few miles from where they were born. Today, very few people expect to stay in the same place throughout their lives.

Why is this important? Because the rate at which our lives are changing means that we have to learn new skills for new jobs. In less than a lifetime, coal mining has gone from being one of the largest employers to one of the smallest, while telephone call centres took a little more than ten years to employ as many people as coal mining once did.

This is why life-long learning is critical for everybody, including team leaders. You need to be ready and willing to learn new skills to take on new tasks and responsibilities. This also means accepting responsibility for your own development. Effective leaders do not expect other people to take responsibility for them, they accept that responsibility themselves.

## Managing your own development

Leadership style, as you have learnt, involves judging when to be 'directive' and when to be supportive. However, you cannot be directive if you don't know what needs to be done. So, you need to be able to set goals, for yourself and for others. You cannot be supportive if you don't know how to communicate with people, motivate them, solve problems or coach new team members. Both 'directive' and supportive leadership styles depend upon you having the right knowledge and skills. To help you to decide which skills you have and which ones you need to develop, fill in the skills assessment questionnaire on pages 50 to 51.

Once you have appraised yourself, you could, if you feel comfortable in doing so, ask your manager and one or two members of your team to do separate ratings. This is called a '360 degree appraisal' or '360 degree feedback' because the appraisal is by the people around you (and there are 360° in a circle).

## Summary

- Leadership style is a combination of how much you direct the team and how much you support it.

- The four main leadership styles are:

  - telling (or authoritarian)

  - selling (or consultative)

  - participating

  - delegating.

- Effective leaders are able to adjust their style to suit the situation.

- Leadership styles depend upon having the right level and mix of skills. Effective team leaders accept some responsibility for developing their own skills. The responsibility starts with recognising what skills they have and which skills they need to develop.

## Review your learning

Look at the descriptions of the four leadership styles.

- Which one do you tend to use most? Is it always the most appropriate style?

- Would you be able to use a wider range of leadership styles if you developed any of the skills you rated yourself as being poor at?

Team leaders need to be ready and willing to learn new skills and to take on new tasks and responsibilities.

# Leadership skills appraisal

## Assess yourself

Use this appraisal to help you to identify which skills you particularly need to develop. You can use your answers to set yourself some personal development goals after you have read the next chapter.

Score each skill by rating yourself as follows.
1.   I am really poor at this.
2.   I am quite bad at this.
3.   I can do this, but should be better at it.
4.   I am quite good at this.
5.   I am really good at this.

### Communication and social skills

| | | | | | |
|---|---|---|---|---|---|
| Explaining things to individuals | 1 | 2 | 3 | 4 | 5 |
| Asking questions and listening to answers | 1 | 2 | 3 | 4 | 5 |
| Talking to groups | 1 | 2 | 3 | 4 | 5 |
| Recognising what people are thinking in the way that they behave | 1 | 2 | 3 | 4 | 5 |

### Goal-setting

| | | | | | |
|---|---|---|---|---|---|
| Setting clear goals for myself | 1 | 2 | 3 | 4 | 5 |
| Achieving my personal goals | 1 | 2 | 3 | 4 | 5 |
| Agreeing clear team goals | 1 | 2 | 3 | 4 | 5 |
| Monitoring how well the team is meeting its goals | 1 | 2 | 3 | 4 | 5 |

### Managing myself

| | | | | | |
|---|---|---|---|---|---|
| Knowing which tasks I have to complete | 1 | 2 | 3 | 4 | 5 |
| Setting a clear timetable for planning my time and completing tasks | 1 | 2 | 3 | 4 | 5 |
| Completing tasks as planned | 1 | 2 | 3 | 4 | 5 |
| Balancing the demands of my job with my personal life | 1 | 2 | 3 | 4 | 5 |

## Motivating people

| | | | | | |
|---|---|---|---|---|---|
| Understanding what motivates different individuals | 1 | 2 | 3 | 4 | 5 |
| Adjusting how I try to motivate individuals according to what I know is appropriate for them | 1 | 2 | 3 | 4 | 5 |
| Bringing out the best in the people I lead | 1 | 2 | 3 | 4 | 5 |

## Being creative in problem-solving

| | | | | | |
|---|---|---|---|---|---|
| Recognising that problems exist and taking action | 1 | 2 | 3 | 4 | 5 |
| Working out what is causing problems | 1 | 2 | 3 | 4 | 5 |
| Involving the team in solving problems | 1 | 2 | 3 | 4 | 5 |
| Encouraging the team to be creative | 1 | 2 | 3 | 4 | 5 |

## Inspiring trust and respect

| | | | | | |
|---|---|---|---|---|---|
| Being open about my attitudes and values, feelings and emotions | 1 | 2 | 3 | 4 | 5 |
| Being open and honest about my expectations and goals | 1 | 2 | 3 | 4 | 5 |
| Always trying to perform as well as I am able | 1 | 2 | 3 | 4 | 5 |
| Asking for help when I need it | 1 | 2 | 3 | 4 | 5 |

## Being interested in and valuing team members

| | | | | | |
|---|---|---|---|---|---|
| Treating team members equally | 1 | 2 | 3 | 4 | 5 |
| Wanting to know about team members' attitudes and values, feelings and emotions | 1 | 2 | 3 | 4 | 5 |
| Wanting to know about team members' expectations and goals | 1 | 2 | 3 | 4 | 5 |
| Celebrating team members' achievements | 1 | 2 | 3 | 4 | 5 |

## Developing the skills of my team

| | | | | | |
|---|---|---|---|---|---|
| Identifying what knowledge and skills team members have | 1 | 2 | 3 | 4 | 5 |
| Identifying which knowledge and skills are needed for different tasks | 1 | 2 | 3 | 4 | 5 |
| Identifying which knowledge and skills team members need to develop | 1 | 2 | 3 | 4 | 5 |
| Training team members | 1 | 2 | 3 | 4 | 5 |
| Coaching team members | 1 | 2 | 3 | 4 | 5 |
| Helping team members to have access to development opportunities (such as training courses) elsewhere | 1 | 2 | 3 | 4 | 5 |

# 9 | Managing yourself effectively

## Introduction

Team leading involves pulling people along behind you, not pushing them, and this involves selecting the appropriate set of skills or leadership style for the particular situation. In Chapter 8 you had a chance to assess your own skills and leadership styles, and you may now have a picture of what you are good at and what you need to improve. In this chapter you have a chance to find out *how* you can make some of these improvements – by managing yourself effectively. This will help you to set goals, plan how to achieve them, use your time wisely and monitor your progress and performance as a team leader.

## Having goals

In Chapter 5 you learnt about SMART team objectives. You can also use SMART goals yourself. SMART stands for **s**pecific, **m**easurable, **a**greed (or **a**chievable), **r**ealistic (or **r**esourced) and **t**imed. Specific means that the goals are clear and unambiguous. Measurable means that you will know whether or not they have been achieved. Agreed, that those who can help or hinder you have agreed them. Realistic, that they are achievable (but the best goals will also *stretch* you to perform to the highest possible standard). Timed means that the goals have clear deadlines.

The British motivational speaker David Taylor says that there are only four steps for guaranteed success in managing your goals.

Step 1: Know where you want to go.

Step 2: Know where you are now.

Step 3: Know what you have to do to get to where you want to go.

Step 4: Do it!

*Know where you want to go*
The first step is *setting* your goals. These are where you want to go or what you want to be. You really have to be clear about what the goals are and you must also really want to achieve them. David Taylor gives the example of people who want to give up smoking. They usually define their goal as giving up smoking, but he argues that is not their goal. Their true goal is to be a non-smoker. People who want to give up smoking are smokers, so their goal is based on where they are, not where they want to be. Being a non-smoker is very different, because it represents the person you want to become, not the person you currently are. It is the destination, not the

journey. So, if you identified one of your weaknesses as 'not involving the team in decision-making', then your goal is to become someone who does involve the team, not to involve them more than you do now. These are very different goals.

### Know where you are now

If we don't know precisely where we are now, then we will not be able to plan the journey accurately. This is why we need to be aware of, and honest about, our own strengths and weaknesses. Only then can we start improving our performance. Sometimes we need confirmation from other people about where we are – help with map reading. So, if you have not yet asked colleagues to appraise you using the questionnaire in Chapter 8, then consider doing so now.

### Know what you have to do to get to where you want to go

"If you do what you have always done you will get where you have always got," says David Taylor. Goals don't get achieved simply by being set. We have to take steps towards them. And if we want to achieve something new, better or more demanding, then we have to take different, bigger steps than we have in the past. Planning how you are going to achieve your goals is often simply about answering five questions.

1. What do I need to do (your goal)?

2. How do I need to do it?

3. When do I need to complete it by?

4. Where will I do it?

5. Who do I need to help, support or allow me to do it?

If you want to involve your team more in making decisions, then your questions and answers could look something like those in the box below.

| What? | Involve the team in decision-making. |
|---|---|
| How? | At weekly team meetings, discuss any significant decisions and agree what we should do. |
| When? | Schedule a team meeting when you know that there is a significant decision to be made, or call a special team meeting if a decision needs to be made quickly. |
| Where? | Meeting room. |
| Who? | All the team members. |

Even where you need to take a series of actions, you can use the five questions to develop an action plan. Just create a table with the five questions at the top (in columns) and the steps down the side (in rows), like the example opposite. The answers become milestones on the road to achieving your main goal, each with a clear date for completion.

### Do it!

Planning is no good without action. No matter how small, take the first step as early as you can and keep on moving towards your goal. Keep your eyes fixed firmly on

## Example of an action plan

**Goal: By next year, to be able to use a computer with confidence**

| What? | How? | When? | Where? | Who? |
|---|---|---|---|---|
| Find out about joining a training course in IT | Speak to someone in the training department | Monday | Head Office | Manager, Training Officer |
| Learn basic IT skills | Attend company's introductory course | By end of next month | Head Office | Manager, Training Officer |
| Use computer to start writing reports | Use computer in the local office | Within two months | Office | Manager |
| Obtain European Computer Driving Licence** | Go on 20 week evening course | Sign up in September | Local adult education centre | Training Officer (will company pay the fee?) |

**Standard European information technology qualification

your goal and remember David Taylor's words: "If you do what you have always done you will get where you have always got." 'Doing it' involves commitment, and commitment means truly believing in what you want to achieve and having the motivation and stamina to see it through. Without commitment, setting goals is pointless. All too often we set goals that we say are committed to, but still do not achieve them because we don't have enough time, are too busy or simply get distracted. Being able to manage your time effectively is the key to the achievement of goals, if you are truly committed to them. If you are not committed, then no amount of time management can help.

## Using your time well

The main reasons we don't achieve what we set out to achieve are:

- the goals are unrealistic
- we don't plan well how to achieve them
- we don't complete our plans because we give up or something interferes with them
- we don't actually start.

## Why don't we have enough time?

In an average week we probably spend about 56 out of 168 hours asleep. If 10 hours are spent travelling to work and another 14 hours eating, then we are left with 88 usable hours on average.

A lot of that remaining time is not free for us to use however we want, because of tasks we have to do at work and chores we have to do at home. However, we do have some choice over *when* we do our tasks and what else we do on top of chores.

If you want to improve your use of time, keep a record (an activity log) for just one week of how you actually spend your time. Make a table with all the hours of the day down the side for each day in the week. Then record what you do during each hour.

At the end of the week total the hours you spend on different types of activity (such as travelling, preparing food, housework, team meetings, talking to neighbours, going to an evening class or taking exercise).

Distinguish between the activities that you have been *directed* to do; those you can *decide when* to do; and those you have *chosen* for yourself. You could also record the tasks you wanted to do but didn't get round to doing because you ran out of time.

Consider whether there are things that take up more or less time than you expected. Are there things you do that you do not need to do? Time management starts with you knowing *how* you use your time, so that you can learn to use it better.

> Time management starts with you knowing *how* you use your time, so that you can learn to use it better.

## Planning tasks

One of the simplest but most effective ways of making better use of your time is to distinguish between tasks that are urgent or important.

Urgent tasks need to be done soon, or immediately, because of one of the following:

- other tasks depend on them
- safety or security is at risk if they are not done soon
- someone has said they *must* be done.

Important tasks have a major effect on other people or tasks. 'Urgency' is about the need for prompt attention, but 'importance' is about the *consequences* the tasks will have. Some urgent tasks are also important, but not all of them.

The chart in the box on page 56 shows you how 'urgency' and 'importance' need to be dealt with.

It may be tempting for the team leader to take on those tasks that seem important. But everyone is important in an effective team, and a good way to develop team members is to encourage them to take on some of the important tasks, with help and support if necessary. This has two benefits:

- it shows that you trust your team to take on the responsibility
- it helps individuals to gain confidence and self-respect.

By sharing out important tasks you help to build a more effective team.

## The urgent/important grid

|  | More urgent | Less urgent |
| --- | --- | --- |
| More important | Needs to be done as soon as any small, urgent but less important tasks are dealt with. | Plan when to do it, allocate time and don't allow yourself to be distracted. Give it your full attention. |
| Less important | These need to be got out of the way immediately. Try delegating them to a team member. If someone has asked you to do it, ask if it really is so urgent. | Does it really need to be done: can someone else do it? If it must be done, save it until it can be done easily without disrupting other work. |

## Procrastination

Procrastination is the tendency to put things off or to allow yourself to be distracted. We all get distracted at times by:

- other people

- other tasks (particularly if someone else says that it is more urgent than the one we are doing)

- our own preferences (if we don't really like doing the task we are doing).

Other people distract you because they have less work to do, are less committed, or need help to do their job. You need to defend your own time from other people who try to steal it from you. If someone in your team is not occupied, then find them tasks to do, delegating some of your tasks if necessary. A time-waster in your team distracts everyone and you need to be firm with someone who avoids work. Challenge people who are not pulling their own weight because they make everyone else work harder as a result. If you have to do something you don't enjoy doing, do not put it off. Instead, reward yourself by doing a task you do enjoy when you've finished it. One way of helping yourself to do this is to prepare a work schedule, or a 'to do' list.

- A work schedule is a detailed list of tasks and times for doing them. If you have a regular pattern of work you can prepare a schedule for each week or each month, then fit other tasks around the scheduled ones. If you prefer some tasks to others, you may be able to schedule the less attractive task before the more attractive, to have something to look forward to.

- A 'to do' list is simply a list of tasks that have to be done. It can help you to identify whether they are urgent or important so that you can work out the best order for doing them. When you complete the task and cross it off the list, you will probably get a sense of achievement.

If other people are trying to affect your decisions about what is urgent or important, especially if it is your manager or a customer, discuss it with them. Ask them why the task is urgent or important. If they have delegated it to you as an urgent task, it may be because they have left it to the last minute and no longer have the time. You may need to explain your own priorities, discuss how best to work together and plan how to tackle recurring activities.

## Take control

The key to achieving your own goals and using your own time effectively is taking control of yourself. Know what you want to achieve, set your priorities for what is urgent and what is important, and then set out towards your goals. That is true in your personal life, in your job and in your career.

Leaders are people who create the conditions in which others are motivated to achieve goals, but the first thing leaders need is the motivation to achieve their own goals. Of course, this is only possible if your goals are realistic, measurable and so on. And what is realistic for one person may not be for another. You must set your goals according to your own circumstances, and then be committed to achieving them, whatever they may be.

## Summary

- Establish a clear picture of where you are now.

- Set your own SMART goals, ensuring that they point you towards what or where you want to be or to do, not what or where you are now.

- Know what you have to do to get to where you want to go by planning effectively. Answer plenty of questions that start with what, how, when, where and who.

- Do it! Distinguish between urgent and important tasks, and don't procrastinate. Use work schedules and 'to do' lists to help you and don't allow other people or tasks to distract you.

## Review your learning

Do you have your own personal and career development goals? If not, what should they be?

Don't finish this chapter without being clear about your goals and how you plan to achieve them. Don't put it off. Do it now!

> The key to achieving your own goals and using your own time effectively is taking control of yourself.

- it can deteriorate in storage so that it must be thrown away or sold off at a loss

- stock costs money to store, and storage areas can be very costly

- if the money used to buy stock has been borrowed, interest has to be paid on it.

However, letting stock levels get too low can disrupt production, waste time and disappoint customers. That is why a balance has to be struck, between too much and too little stock, based on a combination of:

- the minimum order that the supplier will accept

- the time it takes to supply

- the rate at which stock is used.

### Just in time

Some organisations have reduced the ordering period between delivery and low stock levels by using a Just In Time (JIT) system. Parts are ordered to meet production requirements, with nothing held in reserve, and are delivered directly to the production line or cell just when they are needed.


## Understanding the supply chain

JIT relies on partnership arrangements between a customer and its suppliers. They work together to keep production flowing. These partnerships include the suppliers' suppliers, and even their suppliers, who together form the supply chain.

You should know where your organisation and your team's tasks lie in the supply chain. How flexible are your suppliers, how quickly can they supply the products or services your team needs? How many customers are there beyond your team, expecting flexibility and speedy responses from you? Understanding your position in the supply chain helps you to understand how dependent you are on suppliers, and the pressure you may get from your customers.

Even if you work in a service organisation, you may be able to improve the supply chain. Your customers may use their own equivalent of a JIT system – leaving it to the last minute – and expect goods and services to be available the moment they decide they want them. How rapid is the service that your team can provide? Your team needs to recognise how important it is to reduce any delays between the moment when customers place orders and the time when goods or services are delivered. The organisation must match what it supplies to its customers' demands if it is to meet their requirements (and, perhaps, stay in business). Public sector organisations, such as government departments, need to be just as responsive, because service users expect the same quality of service from them that they get elsewhere. Reducing delays, cutting stock levels and being responsive to customers all contribute to improving the team's productivity.


## Improving team productivity

Productivity is another word for efficiency and is generally used when talking about people. Your team's productivity is measured by how much each person produces, or how much the team as a whole produces. It can be improved by:

- increasing team members' skills (see Chapter 15)

- reorganising work patterns and methods (see Chapters 23 and 24)

- identifying barriers to efficient working.

*Identifying barriers to efficient working*
This could be the way that other people in the organisation work or the way that goods or services are supplied to you. You may not be able to change them, but you can tell your manager about the effect on your team's productivity.

## Dealing with poor performers

You may have productivity problems because of the poor performance of a team member. There can be many reasons for this. Team members might be completely out of their depth in the job, unaware that they are not doing what is expected, or suffering from ill health or from personal or family problems.

You should always be prepared to talk to someone who is not performing well and ask if they can identify any reasons. If appropriate, encourage the person to use any services that are available at work (for example in the HR or personnel department) or locally (perhaps they need to consult their doctor) to help them. They may need training or advice on their performance, which you may be able to organise or supply yourself.

If none of this helps, or if they will not acknowledge the problem or respond to what is offered, be prepared to discuss the problem with your manager.

## Monitoring performance

One of your responsibilities as team leader is to monitor your team's performance. This means knowing:

- if all your resources are being used well and fully

- how much is being produced

- whether what is produced meets quality standards.

You and your team are accountable for the way that you use buildings, equipment and consumables. As team leader, you may be responsible for ensuring that team members are present and working to the best of their abilities. This may mean recording and monitoring:

- team members' timekeeping and attendance

- the use and condition of equipment

- the use of consumables and stock levels.

You may also have to record the level of work output and, perhaps, analyse the data for patterns in the team's performance. However, tables of production, absenteeism or faulty goods figures are not easy to analyse or see patterns in. One way of seeing if the data is climbing or falling, or if there is some other pattern over time, is to convert the data to a graph such as the one on page 124.

> Reduce any delays between the moment when customers place orders and the time when goods or services are delivered.

### Interpersonal

Oral and non-verbal communication are together described as interpersonal communication, that is, communication directly between people. Of course, not all communication is directly between people: some is written or recorded and uses channels like the post, radio or the internet.

However, all team leaders need really good interpersonal communication skills even if they do use other channels. Effective interpersonal communication involves making sure that *all* aspects of your communication (the words you use, the way you say them, how you present yourself when you say them) convey the same message.

### Noise

One problem with all the different communication channels is that messages can get distorted by what is called noise. Noise can be any sound that makes it difficult to hear what someone is saying, or anything that distracts receivers from the message. 'Noise' can be in the way that you speak or write, gestures that you use or in the way you present yourself. It can also be poor light or poorly printed materials. The table opposite shows how we use interpersonal communication, the main channels for both oral and non-verbal communication, and some of the common 'noise' that can distort a message.

## Oral communication

Effective communication helps you to share information with others, build relationships within the team and encourage trust between team members. The most important communication channel for any team leader is face-to-face oral communication with team members, either individually or in groups.

Always make an effort to find the most appropriate language – this varies from team to team and often depends on the circumstances. Don't try to use words that you do not understand or would not normally use. The best communicators use simple language in simple sentences, pitched at the level that receivers understand and can hear. Many people tend to use more complicated language when talking formally or to a larger group (such as during a team briefing). This can be as a result of nerves, but it may be because they believe that it is the thing to do. A speaker could, for example, make either of the following two statements.

- "Please clear your desks before leaving work to make it easier for the cleaners."
- "All staff are responsible for ensuring that work surfaces are empty of papers and other materials outside working hours."

Which one do you think would be appropriate and effective when talking to members of your own team, and which when talking to a group of team members and managers? Or would one be clearer in both circumstances?

## Interpersonal communication

| Component | Channel | Noise |
| --- | --- | --- |
| Oral communication (by word of mouth) | Speaking to people face to face, team briefings, formal group presentations, telephone or tele-conferencing | • Poor speaking ability<br>• Misuse of words or using jargon<br>• Sound levels in the immediate environment |
| Non-verbal communication | Tone of voice, facial expression, gesture, posture (how you stand or move), and proximity (how close you are) | • Different cultures interpret different meanings<br>• Unusual gestures<br>• Embarrassment or inexperience at speaking in public<br>• Inappropriate behaviour from the receiver's point of view (touching or standing too close, for example) |

## Non-verbal communication

As we have seen, non-verbal communication is the way we send and receive wordless messages by facial expressions, gaze (see page 65), gestures, posture, proximity or position in relation to other people. It is often called 'body language' (although it is also about tone of voice) because our body communicates our intentions and feelings, irrespective of the words we use. In fact, *how* we say something is often more important than *what* we say. If you are nervous, for example, your voice and facial expression could distract from what you are saying.

# 21 | Keeping the customers satisfied

## Introduction

Only a few staff deal directly with customers, but this does not mean that your team can forget about customers. A key role for team leaders is agreeing standards (or targets) with team members and managers so that you and your team are committed to achieving them. The closer the standards are to customer requirements, the more likely it is that customers will be satisfied with the goods and services they buy or use. This chapter looks at ways you can keep your team members customer-focussed, so that they are committed to meeting and, if possible, exceeding your customers' requirements.

## Who are your customers?

Customers may be external or internal, and may be known by other descriptions such as 'client', 'consumer', 'member' or 'stakeholder'.

### External

External customers are people outside the organisation who buy your organisation's goods and services. They may be individual members of the public (sometimes known as consumers) or they may be other organisations (sometimes called 'B2B' or 'business to business' customers). The other organisations may use the goods and services for themselves or use them to produce other goods and services. (You may know them as 'client organisations'). External customers also include pupils and their parents at a school; patients and their relatives in a hospital; the members of a professional institute; or the donors and beneficiaries of a charity. Even if you do not sell goods and services to them, thinking of them as 'customers' can help you to make their requirements a team priority.

### Internal

It is likely that you have customers inside the organisation too. These internal customers are the people and teams who rely on you and your team to do your team tasks effectively so that they can do theirs. In a factory, for example, a team might carry out one part of the process, before passing the work to other teams for them to complete. In a hospital you might provide cleaning or portering services to ward managers and their staff.

# What do your customers require?

It is the team leader's role to identify your internal and external customers. If you and your team do not deal directly with them, then talk to the people in your organisation who do. Find out what kind of customer buys your organisation's goods and services – old, young, male, female, single, with children, or a small, large local, national, regional or international business.

## How do you know what customers require?

Some organisations spend large amounts of money to find out what their customers require and how they judge quality. If your organisation does this, you may know or be able to find out what has been discovered about your customers. However, there are other ways of finding out, or at least getting a good idea about, what customers require. These include:

- observing customer behaviour
- analysing customer complaints and returns
- collecting feedback
- benchmarking – examining what high-performing (and customer-satisfying) organisations do, comparing this to your organisation's own procedures and making any appropriate changes
- analysing audit and inspection findings.

Ask yourself what your customers *require*. (This avoids debates about whether what they 'want' and what they 'need' are different.) Consider what they are looking for specifically – what it is about your product or service that they will judge it by. These are the quality characteristics. For example, a consumer buying a car may look at its carrying capacity and engine size, colour and trim choices, its 'looks', the car's and the car maker's image (although they may be reluctant to admit to this), the costs of servicing and parts, and the way that sales staff behave.

### Price and quality

Customers are, of course, concerned about price, but their buying decisions are based on how well the products or services match their requirements at a particular price. People usually pay more for something that most closely matches their requirements. Only where all the products and services offered are identical in meeting these requirements will price become the deciding factor.

Price and quality are related, of course. Customers create hierarchies of requirements – an order of priority – with the most important quality characteristics at the top of the hierarchy. This is why a customer who normally buys from a supplier with a slow but cheap delivery may switch to buying from another more expensive supplier selling almost identical items when a fast delivery is needed. Speed has jumped from low to high in the hierarchy of requirements, displacing cost.

The ideal situation to be in is to be able to meet a customer's requirements fully, to offer all the preferred quality characteristics and to be able to compete on price. This is where standards and teams come in.

> Ask yourself what your customers *require.*

# 11 | Developing your communication skills

## Introduction

As a team leader you need to be able to communicate effectively with your team, your manager, your customers and your suppliers. Chapter 10 introduced the basic principles of communication and the various channels you can use. This chapter will help you to develop your skills in asking questions, listening and giving and accepting feedback.

## Effective interpersonal communication

As you saw in Chapter 10, interpersonal communication combines oral (spoken) and non-verbal communication.

## Clarity

Good communication involves you in speaking clearly, asking questions, listening carefully and using appropriate language for the people and circumstances. You need to suit what you say to the particular listeners. If people are unfamiliar with your accent, for example, they may struggle to make sense of what you are saying. You can usually judge whether your accent is a barrier to communication if people ask you to repeat what you say or seem to mishear you regularly. If they do, you need to make your comments clearer for them.

You should also take care about using slang or jargon, because they can add to 'noise' in your communication. Slang is informal language which is not always appropriate (when talking to customers or suppliers, for example) and which some people might even find to be offensive. Jargon is the language of specialists. It often includes technical terms, which are impossible for non-specialists to understand. Use jargon only with the people with the right level of knowledge.

## Letting your body 'speak'

As you saw in Chapter 10, *how* you say something is as important as *what* you say. So, you may want to consider the following points.

### Tone of voice
*How* you speak can affect how well people understand you. If they react badly, it could be because you sound critical. (If people react in a way you had not expected,

ask someone you trust what they think of your tone and whether you show your feelings or intentions clearly in how you speak.)

### Gaze

'Gaze' is where people look when they talk, in particular whether the speaker looks you in the eye. Frequent eye contact (but not staring) when you are listening shows that you are interested in what someone is saying. Always avoid looking past someone, as if you are interested in something else. When talking to a group of people, run your gaze around the whole group and avoid looking at only a particular individual or group, as it can seem that you are talking only to them.

### Facial expression

Many of these occur instinctively and are interpreted in the same way around the world. A smile, for instance, is the same everywhere. You often know how someone is feeling from the expression on his or her face. This is because the face is one of the ways we show emotions. Don't be afraid to show emotion if it helps to reinforce what you are saying.

### Gestures

We use our hands to emphasise meaning and to indicate locations and directions – even when we are on the telephone and the person at the other end cannot see them. Don't be afraid to use gestures, especially when you are speaking to a group, because they can help to make your message clearer.

### Posture

When you sit down, try leaning forward and looking someone directly in the eye, without staring. You then emphasise that you are giving that person your full attention. People may not recognise what you are doing, but they will still be affected by your posture. Watch other people and you will start to recognise when their posture matches or emphasises what they are saying and when it does not.

### Proximity

We all like to have some space around us: when someone gets too close, it can feel like an invasion. You may be the kind of person who does not like to touch other people, or to be touched. Alternatively, you may feel that it is perfectly natural to put your arm around someone's shoulders or to hold their arm as you talk to them, and that it emphasises your words. Be aware of how other people feel, because you could cause offence, or find yourself accused of harassment. Proximity can also be used to show power, as powerful people sometimes invade 'personal space' at will.

## Using your communication skills

When you are trying to communicate with someone in person, you employ a range of oral communication techniques, backed up by non-verbal signals. The main skills you need as a team leader are the ability to:

- ask questions
- listen actively
- inform and persuade
- give and receive feedback.

> Look for ways to improve what you do, so that you continuously raise standards.

with the goods and services they buy or use – provided that those standards are achieved. To match your team's performance standards as closely as possible to customer requirements, you and the team should:

- find out what (internal or external) customers require – this may involve collaboration with other people or teams

- set standards or targets that reflect those requirements and that you believe you can achieve

- work to achieve those standards and targets consistently

- look for ways to improve what you do, so that you continuously raise standards.

As a team leader, this is where you can make one of your most important contributions and help your team to become a high-performing one. The next chapter looks at how you can create a team that is responsive to customer needs and able to produce the goods and services they require.

## Summary

- Your team should satisfy the requirements of its external customers and internal customers as far as is possible.

- Customers judge your organisation's goods and services against sets of quality characteristics that reflect their requirements. The requirements have different priorities and may vary from time to time.

- You, your team and your organisation can identify customer requirements and set measurable, achievable standards to satisfy them.

- Your team needs goals and standards/targets to define what you are aiming to achieve in order to meet customers' requirements. They are what you, your team and your organisation measure your performance against.

- Being customer-focussed involves identifying what customers require, setting and consistently achieving standards that reflect those requirements, and looking for ways to improve performance and raise standards.

## Review your learning

- Who are your internal and external customers?

- How do you know what they require? Who do you need to speak with in the organisation, and what methods for finding out customer requirements might be most appropriate for your sector, organisation and team?

- What standards or targets do you work to? How well do these reflect customers' requirements and priorities?

- How well do you achieve these standards or targets?

- How can you involve team members more in setting and achieving customer requirements?

# 22 | Creating a flexible team

## Introduction

Teams can bring flexibility to the way goods and services are produced, so that they meet customers' requirements more closely. This chapter considers the advantages to an organisation of having teams that can work flexibly and shows how flexible working is often part of a technique called 'cell' (or 'zone') working.

## Flexible production

People have become far choosier about what they buy. They want goods and services that meet their specific requirements. Until mass production arrived, most goods and services used to be produced for individual customers in a craft or jobbing production system. Mass production changed all this as very large factories produced identical products in huge volumes at much lower cost than a craft system could achieve. Now craft or jobbing production tends to be used only with high-value items where customers can afford to pay for something exclusive, such as designer clothes, or where the market is small, as with building power stations, for instance. Mass production is now the norm.

Many people want products and services that suit them personally, as if they were produced just for them, but at mass production prices. This has led to the process of 'mass customisation', where standard products are produced with large numbers of variations that can be included as the product or service is produced. Cars coming down the same production line can all be fitted with different equipment and be different colours, each one slightly different from the one in front and the one behind. A travel firm can put together holiday packages comprising different flights, different locations, car hire and other extras, all based on standard services.

### Mass customisation at Dell

Dell revolutionised the market for personal computers (PCs) by not holding any stock of finished products. Each computer is made to order, using standard components. The customers decide which of the different parts they want in their machine and these are then combined and the PC is despatched. Dell also holds as few stocks of components as the company dares. Each time a customer decides on a particular component, this is allocated from stock and, when the number falls to a particular level, replacements are ordered. This also helps to keep costs down.

*Having an alert posture*

Sitting or standing up straight, perhaps even leaning slightly towards the speaker, also indicates that you are paying attention (without being overbearing).

*Acknowledging what they say*

Comments like "Really?", "I know!" or just "Mmm" help to confirm that you are paying attention. You can also reflect back what they have said, summarising their comments in your own words. This helps you to remember and helps them to confirm that you have understood correctly.

## Inform and persuade

These two skills are different but closely related.

*Informing*

Informing is the main purpose of communication. There are some simple steps you can use to help you to pass on information that you want people to remember.

### Start with what people already know

Think of memory as being like a row of coat hooks. We need to find the right hook to hang a new piece of information on. If you want, for example, to tell a team member that an existing customer has placed another order, try saying, "You remember Mr Parsons who had that large order last month? Well, he has ordered…"

### Number points and work through them in turn

"There are three things you need to remember when you use that machine. One, …. If there are a lot of points, then group them as 'chunks' of information. If, for example, there are ten things to remember when using a machine, group them into 'starting', 'running' and 'clearing up', with three or four points under each heading.

### Summarise at the end

If the information is complex, then it sometimes helps to start with a brief introduction, then give the details, and at the end give a concluding summary – for example, "OK, so it's prime, clutch and start."

### Check understanding

A good way to do this is to ask the person to run through the main points. If the person has forgotten or misunderstood, use hints or give another explanation. Remember, if they have got it wrong, it is your responsibility to ensure that they get it right.

*Persuading*

Persuasion is used to bring about a change in deeply held attitudes or set ways of behaving. To persuade people you need to be very clear about what they currently think or do and try to work with them rather than argue against them. If, for example, you want team members to be less wasteful in using materials, you will be successful only if they accept that reducing wastage is worthwhile. If they believe that the company wastes other resources, so it does not matter what they do, then you will probably fail. Suit your persuasion to the people you want to persuade, not to fit your own values or beliefs. For example, you could try persuading them about the ecological benefits of less waste if they are keen on environmental matters.

## Give and receive feedback

Feedback is information about something that someone has done. Giving and receiving feedback is an excellent way of developing your own and your team's performance. It helps everybody to learn what they are doing well and how they need to improve.

Giving feedback is a key part of your role. It relies on your ability to communicate with other people – how you give information, ask questions, listen and observe body language. Like most skills, giving feedback improves only through practice, so you should always be looking for opportunities to try out your communication skills and to give and receive feedback.

### Giving feedback

You can encourage your colleagues to develop the things they do well by giving positive feedback. This includes simply saying 'well done', as well as giving more structured comments. You can give negative feedback to help your colleagues to improve the things they do *not* do well, or which cause problems for other people. This should not be a 'telling off'. All effective feedback involves you in identifying areas where improvements could be made. People often do things badly because they just do not know what they should do differently.

When giving feedback you need to think how the person will feel, and try to balance negative and positive feedback, perhaps by mentioning the things they do well before pointing out what they need to do better. The one exception is where behaviour is likely to be unsafe, cause significant problems or lead to formal disciplinary procedures. Then an immediate and clear warning is needed.

Whenever you give feedback, always say what you have *seen*, not what you think people were *intending* or *thinking*. If you say, for example, "You weren't thinking about the dangers to other people", you imply that you are a mind reader and will not get to the root of the problem. If you say, "What you did could have caused serious injury to other people" it is far more to the point. You could then follow that up by asking, "Were you thinking about the possible danger at the time?"

### Receiving feedback

If you want people to value your feedback, it helps to show that you welcome it yourself. However, you have to show that you want serious, constructive feedback and are not simply inviting your team to tell you how good you are. Invite team members to give their comments on how you perform a particular task. You can also ask your manager for feedback. This is called a '360 degree feedback' because it comes from all around you, like the 360° in a circle.

> You need to stay in touch with team members, even if it is just to confirm that all is going as planned.

## Staying in touch

You need to stay in touch with team members, even if it is just to confirm that all is going as planned. Regular, low-key communication helps to build relationships and understanding between people, and strengthens your team. You also need to maintain contact with people outside your team, especially those who you do not see often. Occasional chats or a short email show that you are interested. However, if you make contact only when you need help, people may dread your calls or visits.

# 23 | Is there a problem?

## Introduction

It is crucial for teams to have clear standards for their work that reflect what internal or external customers require. Despite your best efforts, however, there may be times when you and your team encounter problems in achieving those standards. This chapter looks at ways to monitor your performance, find out what is causing a problem and what you and your team can do about it.

## When things go wrong

Problems that could stop the team from meeting customer requirements include:

- late delivery of essential materials, parts or services

- a breakdown or wrong setting on equipment

- sickness or absenteeism among team members

- poor performance among some team members, due to insufficient skills, a lack of commitment or motivation, or personal problems

- an emergency or crisis that could not be forecast, such as power failure, fire or flood.

When these or other problems occur, you need to distinguish between those that you and your team can do something about and those that are outside your control.

### What can the team do something about?

**Problems you can do something about yourselves**

- Poor operation of equipment

- Lack of skill

- Poor relationships in the team

- Tasks wrongly allocated

- Team members not knowing what is expected of them

**Problems you need other people to do something about**

- Suppliers badly selected

- Badly designed production systems in the organisation

- Poorly made products and low standard services bought for your team to use

- Emergencies or crises, like power failures or snowdrifts

You should concentrate the team's energies on the problems they can do something about. Some problems may need you to bring together all the people involved, perhaps as a quality circle (see page 21). If the problem lies with an external supplier, then the team responsible there could be invited to discuss the problem with your team.

## Monitoring performance

Some problems are immediately obvious – like a breakdown of machinery. Others can be prevented if there are systems of feedback in place to alert you in good time. Feedback is information flowing back to you about your actions (see page 69). The feedback could be informal, such as a customer complaint by phone, or a formal system for collecting data on performance as part of the quality control of products and services.

Quality control is the system to ensure that products and services are to the desired standard. It consists of four steps.

1. Set standards (and targets) for performance.

2. Monitor performance to check what is being produced or supplied.

3. Compare what is produced against the standards.

4. Take action if performance fails to meet the standards.

### Set standards
Standards and targets (see Chapter 21) describe the quality of the product or service that the team should produce or supply consistently to meet customer requirements.

### Monitor performance
Monitoring (see pages 123-124) may include observation, automatic data collection or the keeping of records of what the team has done and how effective it was.

### Compare output with standards
By collecting data and analysing them, the team can identify when things are going wrong. The basis for any analysis should be what you intended to do – your standards.

### Take action
The whole point of quality control is to do something. Without action the previous three stages are a waste of time and effort.

> You should concentrate the team's energies on the problems they can do something about.

## Effective monitoring systems

A good monitoring system needs to balance all three of the following:

- low cost (because resources should be spent on *doing* not measuring)

- validity (so that it can measure what it is important to measure)

- promptness (so that you get feedback as soon as possible and can take action fast).

## The purpose of team briefings

If team briefings are done well, messages are passed on more accurately and completely than by any other channel of communication in an organisation. Given that, why are they not used more? Partly it is a question of trust. There is a famous story that during the First World War an officer told his men to pass a message down the line to the signaller to send back to headquarters (HQ). The message was, "Send reinforcements, am going to advance." By the time the message reached HQ it read, "Send three and fourpence, I'm going to a dance." Unlikely? Possibly, but it demonstrates why managers are always worried that messages will be changed or distorted as they are passed on.

So, in giving team briefings, you need to:

- be very clear about the message you need to send
- check that it has been received clearly and understood.

### Several-way process

Team briefings enable all the team members to ask questions, raise issues or air problems. It is your responsibility to ensure that you can answer all their likely questions accurately, or that you find out an answer and report back to them as quickly as possible. You also need to pay attention to the points that team members raise, as you may need to pass aspects of those points on to people outside the team, especially if it could affect the outcomes of a planned activity.

As well as enabling you to pass on information from the senior managers, briefings allow you to communicate information from your line manager, other teams and other sources. Typical topics that benefit from being presented through team briefings include training and development opportunities, planned maintenance on equipment, new team members starting, holiday or shift changes, new products or services, promotions and team performance results.

In some teams the members take it in turns to bring in biscuits or cakes, which helps to build the sense of being part of a team. The briefing can also be a chance for individual members to pass on information or give feedback on an activity. This also helps to build the team and emphasises that the team leader is not the only person who has useful or important information. It can also be used to recognise a team member who has done something useful or performed particularly well. There may even be a system of rewards for individuals who hit targets, although this can be divisive if the same people win frequently.

## Planning a team briefing

A team briefing can be a one-off event or could happen every week, or even every day. It doesn't matter which, there is always the same need to plan it properly. Planning starts by being clear about the purpose of the briefing:

- what information you want the team to know
- what action you want the team members to take.

> If team briefings are done well, messages are passed on more accurately and completely than by any other channel of communication in an organisation.

These are two separate issues. The fact that the IT system will be down overnight, for instance, may be just something for them to *know*. That they should switch off their machines at the end of the day's work (and not just log off from the server as usual) is something they must *do*.

## Sequence

You should then sort the topics for the briefing into order. Remember the urgent/important grid (see page 56) and deal with important matters first, because putting them first emphasises their importance. Then deal with the least important items, and finish with the most urgent, so that you can leave the team members at the end thinking about what needs to be done urgently. This means that the ideal order for topics is as follows.

1. Most important issues – team members must know or do this.

2. Useful but less important details – team members should know or do this.

3. Urgent issues – team members must do this soon or straight away.

You should 'top and tail' your briefing with a summary. It is useful to remember the following three simple steps.

Step 1: Tell them what you are going to say (introduction).

Step 2: Say it (important, useful, urgent).

Step 3: Tell them what you have said (summary).

# Presenting your briefing

A briefing is neither a formal presentation nor a speech. You will probably need to make notes to ensure that you cover all the relevant points. But avoid writing every word beforehand, if you can, and leave the actual words until you are facing the team. That way you ensure that you maintain eye contact (because you are not reading) and will sound as if you mean what you are saying.

If you have prepared for the briefing properly, you will have made a plan. This will start with Step 1 (above) – a short summary of the issues you will cover, in the order you will cover them. In Step 2 you will list each item again, with the key points you should cover, clearly identifying any action that team members need to take. Remember to start with the most important and finish with the most urgent. In Step 3, note down the list again to use as a final summary. If something needs to be done straight away, you should emphasise this as the final point – the most urgent – so that it is the last thought in everyone's mind as they leave. The example in the box over the page gives you an idea what your briefing notes could look like.

If you already give regular team briefings, check that you are preparing them carefully, that you cover topics in the best order and everyone knows what they have to do. If you do not have regular team briefings, try organising an occasional one, discussing with your manager what the team needs to know and how you can contribute to the organisation's communications.

## Getting started

Before you start the briefing, particularly if it is a regular one, it can be useful to start with an 'ice-breaker'. This will help people to stop thinking about whatever they have just been doing and concentrate on the briefing. Ice-breakers range from finding out how their day has been, to doing a Mexican wave! Some teams use this as a chance for sharing personal information, especially at team briefings first thing on Monday mornings.

## Team briefing note

**Team meeting: 3.30pm Friday 29 August**

Introduction

1. New team member starting

2. Clear desks for cleaners

3. System close-down

Details

1. New team member starting

    a. Peter Tilling starts Monday

    b. Joan will be his buddy

    c. Just left college, will need help

    d. Induction with HR lasts until Wed

2. Clear desks for cleaners

    a. Every night – facilities department will be checking

    b. Security and confidentiality of information

    c. Risk of losing important documents

    d. Cleaners will not clean desks if not clear

3. System close-down

    a. New computer system installed

    b. All machines switched off for the weekend

Summary

1. New team member starting (IMPORTANT)

2. Clear desks for cleaners

3. System close-down (URGENT)

Recap
- What have you all to do before we leave today? (Switch off computers.)
- What should you do at the end of every day? (Clear desks.)

## Concluding the briefing

A team briefing is not just about giving information. It is also about getting things done. Check that your team members have understood what they have to do. Ask them questions to check they understand. It might help to make a joke about it, but at least you will know that they understand and remember what you have told them.

## Leaders as communication channels

A team briefing is an essential part of your organisation's communication system. As a team leader, you can be the channel for some of the most important information that passses between managers and team members. By planning how best to pass on information, and by listening as well as talking, you can make this an effective and 'noise'-free channel that everyone values.

## Summary

- Team leaders must plan their briefings. They must be clear what it is they want their teams to know and what they want them to do as a result of the briefing.

- The best order for items to be covered in the briefing is to start with the most important, then cover useful information and finish with the most urgent.

- The best structure for a team briefing is the following sequence.

  - Step 1:    Tell them what you are going to say.

  - Step 2:    Say it.

  - Step 3:    Tell them what you have said.

- Briefings should be informal. Use notes to ensure that you cover all the necessary points, but don't read them as a speech.

## Review your learning

If you do not use team briefings, consider whether there is any benefit from using them. Talk to your manager about the value of team briefings as a way for the organisation to communicate with teams, and consider how you could develop this communication channel.

If you already use team briefings to communicate with your team, review how you do it. Do you:

- plan and prepare for the briefings?

- have a clear structure and put items in an order that reflects their importance and urgency?

- check that team members have understood what they have been told and know what they have to do?

You can be the channel for some of the most important information that passses between managers and team members.

# Developing the team

The best teams have members who are skilled, committed to the team, goal-focussed, flexible and motivated. Above all, they are well led. In Sections One and Two you read about teams, leadership and communication. Now it is time to pull it together to help you to build a high-performing team, in which members can perform to the highest level they are capable of achieving.

What singles out high-performing teams is that their team members regard the team and its performance as being more important than their own personal roles and performances. Even so, a team is still made up of individuals who have their own personalities, attitudes, needs and responsibilities. Welding these different people into a team is not easy, which is why one of the most important aspects of the team leader role is to understand people and to get them all working together as a team. Section Three looks at what is involved.

The section starts by looking at how best to help new team members to become effective, and some of the barriers that they might face. It also outlines the important role that team leaders have in ensuring that team members have, or acquire , the necessary skills.

In an increasingly diverse society, team leaders need to ensure that diversity adds to their team's effectiveness. Suggestions are given about how to stay alert to some of the problems that can occur, and what action to take if they do arise.

Finally, this section looks at the benefits of creative disagreements among team members and the problems of unhealthy emotional conflicts that reduce the team's effectiveness. Suggestions are offered about ways that team leaders can prevent conflict, what to do if conflict does occur and how best to respond to disciplinary issues.

# 13 | Supporting new team members

## Introduction

Team leaders should aim to develop a high-performing team, but this can present problems when new members join, unless their induction into the team is properly organised. This chapter looks at the problems faced by new team members and what team leaders can do to overcome them. It also looks at the role that other team members can have in helping new members to settle so they can play a worthwhile part in the team as quickly as possible.

## Why new people join teams

New people usually join an established team because of one of the following:

- someone has left the team
- the team's responsibilities have changed and more people are needed.

Teams are as much about social relationships (how well people like, trust and respect one another) as they are about work relationships (the tasks people perform together). New people have to build new social relationships and also demonstrate that they can be relied on to perform tasks well, or are willing and able to learn how to do them.

Effective teams are similar to groups of friends, and it can be quite stressful when a team member leaves, like a friend moving away. There are often ceremonies to mark the leaver's departure, with cards, presents and parties, and often a sense of 'mourning'. (Of course, some team members are seen off with a sigh of relief from the rest, but the high-performing teams tend not to have such members.) The strength of the team can also make it rather exclusive: imagine what it's like for someone joining a really effective team after a long-term member has left (see box on following page).

### Replacing team members

A replacement team member must not be expected to be the member who has left. The new member may well take on the task role of the departing member, but that doesn't also mean taking on the team role too. As team leader, it is your responsibility to think about the different roles played by the person who has left and to look at ways of sharing out the roles differently, based on the strengths of the team as it now is. You may have to wait until the person has started before you can fully appreciate what he or she has to offer. You also need to discourage other team members from making comparisons between the new and the old team member. New team members should be judged on how well they perform their tasks, not how they compare to the previous team member.

## Unreasonable expectations

Sally Parsons was one of a seven-person team that had been together for nearly nine years. When she was offered a wonderful promotion opportunity her team colleagues celebrated her promotion and said farewell with a big party. The following working day Tim Allen joined the team. Other members of the team referred to him as the 'new Sally' and expected him to take on some of Sally's social responsibilities (her team role) as well as her work tasks (her task role). Sally was outgoing and lively, but Tim was quiet, thoughtful and conscientious. In many ways he did the task role better than Sally, who could be a bit slapdash at times. However, he could not perform her exact social role, and so felt under pressure when constantly reminded of what 'Sally would have done'.

## Expanding the team

If the team needs to grow bigger, new team members will have new roles, which may be straightforward, but could prove to be a problem. The major difficulty is the division between the old team and the new. The old team can form into a tight-knit 'team within a team' that excludes new team members from decision-making and from social activities. New members may be expected to do the worst or the least valued jobs and be treated like second-class members.

This treatment may have nothing to do with the new team members' personal traits or behaviour. What the old team is trying to do is to hold on to its old team identity. It has formed such a strong sense of being a team that members cannot cope with the new team being bigger than the old one. As a team leader, you need to make sure that the old team is replaced by the new. In effect, you need to go through the process of forming the team all over again.

# Re-forming, re-storming, re-norming, performing

In Chapter 4 you learnt about the way that teams are formed. Every time the team changes its membership you should treat it as a *new* team. Encourage the team to look at what each member does and how the team members work together. Tasks can be shared out differently and people can work together in different ways. In the process, the contribution of new team members can be assessed and they can be encouraged to take on roles that suit them, not those of previous team members or all the unpopular tasks. As team leader, you need to:

- re-form – by bringing the new team members together, reviewing the team goals and which tasks people should perform

- re-storm – by looking at different ways of working that might be more effective in raising quality, increasing output or improving efficiency

- re-norm – by establishing new ways of working and new standards of performance

- perform – as a *new* team.

This doesn't have to be a major upheaval. Introduce the new team member by, for example, reviewing team goals and how the team achieves them. Over the next week or so (once new team members have started to settle into the team, but before they get too fixed into their roles) ask the existing team members how to change the way things work. Some techniques for doing this are covered in Chapters 23 and 24.

## Inducting new team members

So far we have been looking at what you need to do to ensure that the team responds well to a new team member, but you have an important role to play in helping the new team member to settle in quickly. This process is called induction. (The word comes from the Latin for 'to lead into'.)

Some organisations have formal inductions that can last for a few days, perhaps spread over several months. Others have nothing formal and rely on team leaders and others to 'organise something'. Whichever your organisation uses, you should understand what induction is for, what a good induction should do and what part you can play in bringing it about.

### Why induct new team members?

There has been plenty of research that shows that new team members can contribute very little when they first start working, despite the skills they have. What can make all the difference is:

- how quickly they settle in to the new role

- how well they learn the things that are specific to the organisation and the team

- how motivated they can become by the reception the team gives them.

Induction should be designed to speed up the process by which new team members settle in, learn the specific details that they need and feel some personal responsibility for achieving the team's goals.

### What should a good induction be like?

A good induction should provide new team members with the information they need to work effectively. The trouble is, if they are told everything at once, then they will remember very little of it. A good induction lets people know what is immediately crucial and shows them how to find out about other things they may need to know. The induction should gradually give more information. Once they have settled in, they are better able to absorb what they are told and to ask relevant questions.

A good induction lets people know what is immediately crucial and shows them how to find out about other things they may need to know.

## What should a good induction cover?

The range of issues that should be covered in a particular induction vary from job to job, but should generally cover this list.

## Induction issues

| Employment issues | Team and task issues | Personal issues |
|---|---|---|
| • Organisation mission, values and business objectives | • Team structure, members and their roles | • Role and tasks |
| • Organisation structure and management roles | • Team goals | • Training or coaching arrangements |
| • Employment policies and procedures (such as, equal opportunities, harassment and disciplinary procedures) | • Team communications, team meetings and briefings | • Work area (such as, desk) |
| | • Product and service details, work tasks, and procedures | • Equipment, tools and materials |
| • Employment contract details (such as, hours of working, pay, holiday entitlement and pension) | • Quality standards and monitoring procedures | • Work facilities (such as, canteen, refreshments, lockers and changing areas) |
| | • Health, safety and environmental protection | • Security pass or identity card |
| • Appraisal, and training and development procedures and opportunities | | |
| • Trade union membership, works councils and other representation arrangements | | |

Employment issues are those relating to the organisation and the terms and conditions of employment. They need to be covered during induction because not everyone takes in every detail discussed at a job interview or provided in the documents sent out with the job offer.

Team and task issues are specific to the team, and help new members to understand how the team operates and where they fit into it.

Personal issues are those specific to the individual, and cover what the person needs to know to do the job. Together, these are the most urgent and the most important issues that new team members need to know about and understand.

# The leader's role in inducting new team members

You are likely to be involved in the team, the task and the personal aspects of the induction. These may be your sole responsibility as team leader, or you may share the responsibility with your line manager or with specialists in your human resources, personnel or training departments. Take your responsibilities seriously, because this is your opportunity to make sure that new team members learn what is important and how to do things properly. In particular, you can make sure that new members do not bring in any bad habits from previous jobs or, if these are new roles, that they do not make mistakes because of their ignorance or lack of skill.

## New team members and changes

If you are unhappy with some aspect of the way that the team works, don't try to change it by getting the new team member to do it differently. This is unfair and unwise. If you do this, the rest of the team will put pressure on the new member to conform to the way that they do things now, and it is very hard for someone new to resist that pressure. All you will do is to cause a lot of stress for the new team member and waste your time.

If you want everyone to change, you need to work with the whole team, not just someone new.

## Involving the team

You don't have to lead the whole induction yourself. In fact, it is better for the team if you do not. One way is to ask another team member to be a buddy for the new team member.

A buddy is someone who can advise, guide and encourage new team members so that they have someone to rely on and to keep an eye on them. (A buddy is sometimes called a 'mentor', but true mentors have a far bigger role than buddies.) Buddying is one of the team roles that help members to build the team. Buddies should be chosen to fit the new person and his or her needs. It can be useful to match them by sex, age or ethnicity, but they should have the right knowledge and skills to be able to give task-related help as well as personal help.

You also need to make sure that the buddy appreciates how important the role is. The person you choose should be prepared to play an active part for the first few weeks, checking that the new team member has fitted in well and has no problems with any of the other team members, the task or personal issues. Gradually the role lessens until the new member is obviously a confident member of the team. This may take only a few weeks with some people, but younger or less confident people might need some continuing support for several months.

### Coaching

You can also call on other team members to coach new members. (Coaching is covered in more detail in Chapter 15.) It can be used to help new team members to learn specific knowledge or acquire skills that they need in order to perform their role, and is a useful way of sharing the skills and knowledge of experienced members of the team. It is also another way that existing members of the team can play a part in building the team, by recognising that they have skills that are valued and which can be used to help others to meet the standards required.

## Planning a new team member's induction

When a new member is about to join the team, put together an induction plan, with the help of the rest of the team. Between you, you will need to decide:

- what needs to be covered
- which sequence (in what order) to cover them
- how the issues are best covered
- who is best able to cover them in that way.

### What needs to be covered

Start by identifying what you think the new team member needs to learn about the team, their role in it and the other relevant issues.

### Which sequence to cover them

Work out the order in which these things should be introduced, remembering the urgent/important grid (page 56). Some things need to be learnt urgently, such as where the toilets are or what the health and safety rules are. People don't always remember everything they learn on their first day. Cover simple but useful things first that will enable the person to get started. Leave important things until a bit later, when the new team member can concentrate better.

### How they are best covered

Having decided the topics and their sequence, then decide how best to cover them. This could be a guided tour, a one-to-one chat or a questionnaire for which the new team member has to find out all the answers.

### Who is the best person to be involved

You and the team need to decide who is the best person to take responsibility for each topic or group of topics. For example, you might ask a buddy to explain certain issues, you might ask another team member to be a coach to help to develop some specific skills, and you might ask the quality manager and the health and safety officer to cover specialist areas.

### Reviewing the process

Once team members have had a chance to settle in, ask them for their feedback on the effectiveness of their induction, and be prepared to make changes next time if you have not got everything right this time. Take the opportunity to check that new team members have absorbed all the things they need to, have done all they need to, and know how to get help and advice when they need it.

## Summary

- When new people join the team, either replacing someone who has left or adding to the team, the team often needs to be rebuilt.

- A planned induction can help a new team member to perform more effectively, more quickly.

- When planning induction it may help to separate topics under the headings of team, task and personal issues.

- You can use other team members as mentors or coaches to help you to induct new team members, as well as asking specialists from outside the team.

## Review your learning

Look at the list of issues usually covered by inductions on page 80.

- Which of these would (or should) you normally have responsibility for covering when a new member joins the team?

- Which of these would best be covered by other members of the team acting as:

  - mentors?

  - coaches?

- What does the team do to check that new team members are settling in, are comfortable with their roles and performing to the best of their ability?

> You don't have to lead the whole induction yourself. In fact, it is better for the team if you do not.

# 14 | Carrots, not sticks

## Introduction

What makes people 'tick'? What is it that gets them up in the morning to come to work? And what gets them performing well or badly once there? These questions are about motivation – what causes people to be committed to the team, to work co-operatively, to develop their own skills and to help other people to develop theirs. It is motivation that gets people championing quality improvement and wanting to achieve stretch goals. In other words, without motivation, there would be no high-performing teams.

Motivating teams is one of the major skills that team leaders need to develop. This chapter looks at some of the theories of motivation to see what they can suggest for ensuring that your team's members all perform as well as they are able.

## What is motivation?

Motivation is the desire or willingness to do something. It is a personal drive, made stronger or weaker by our reaction to the people we work with and the work we do. Where we work, what it is like physically, the behaviour of the people we work with, our conditions of employment and pay rates can all make us feel more motivated or less motivated to work well.

As a team leader you have responsibility for encouraging members of your team to reach and exceed their capabilities. But there are limits to what you can do. You do *not* control team members' wages or conditions of service, their hours and holiday entitlement, or decide where they work. What you can do is to try to create an environment (how people get on with each other) that makes team members feel motivated to work as well as they are able. You can allocate tasks and arrange workloads to make team members feel that at the very least they are not being given worse conditions than others. You can enable people to have some say in their work, you can make them feel more in control of their working life and you can encourage others by being positive and enthusiastic about getting tasks done. However, before looking in detail at what you might be able to do, it's worth considering some ideas about the nature and causes of motivation.

## The hierarchy of needs

One of the foundations for understanding motivation at work was developed by the American behavioural psychologist Abraham Maslow. He concluded that we are driven by certain needs and these needs are in a hierarchy, or order of importance, that can be represented by a pyramid (see box opposite).

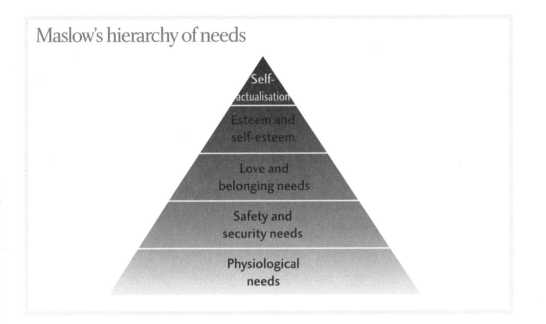

## Maslow's hierarchy of needs

Self-actualisation

Esteem and self-esteem

Love and belonging needs

Safety and security needs

Physiological needs

### The first four levels of need

At the bottom of Maslow's hierarchy of needs are some essentials for human survival, such as oxygen, water, food, avoidance of pain and other such physiological needs for physical well-being.

When these needs are more or less taken care of, then we are motivated by our need for safety and security, the need for shelter from the weather and protection from any threats.

But humans are social animals and, once we are safe and secure, we start to feel lonely. The third level of need is for love and belonging, the need to spend time with other people.

However, it is not enough simply to have friends. What we really want is for our friends and acquaintances to respect us. We also want to feel self-respect. So the fourth layer in the hierarchy of needs is the need for esteem.

If any of these four levels of need (physiological, safety and security, love and belonging, and esteem) are not met, we really miss them. But once they have been met, we can almost forget about them. If you are really hungry, this need becomes dominant, but if you have just eaten, it is quite hard to even think about food. The motivation has disappeared. What's more, within the first four layers of needs, a lower level of need tends to override a higher level one. If you are starving, for example, you will probably forget what anybody else might think of you and might not even care about your own self-respect.

### The fifth layer of need

However, the fifth and top level of motivation is different. This is self-actualisation – the need to achieve what you believe you are really capable of, to fulfil your potential. It is self-actualisation that leads people to get up at five in the morning to spend three hours swimming in a public pool before work to become Olympic champions, that leads people to spend long hours studying to gain qualifications, that makes people work hard for charities for no financial reward.

Why is self-actualisation different? Because it is almost impossible to fulfil this need. It is a need that drives people into extreme feats of achievement but still leaves them wanting to do more. It is what makes people who seem to have achieved their ambitions simply revise those ambitions. We can be well fed, safe, well liked and respected and self-assured, yet still feel the need to do more.

## Motivation at work

How can the hierarchy of needs help you to understand how people might behave? If, for example, team members are feeling hungry (say just before lunch), you might find their motivation to work diminishes. If there is a rumour of job losses, they mighty feel insecure and unwanted, reducing their commitment to the job.

More importantly, the model suggests that many features of being in a team, such as a sense of belonging and being respected for your contribution, are important in motivating people. If the lowest-level needs are not satisfied, then people might not try to fulfil their highest level of need, self-actualisation, and might not get near to achieving their full potential. So, working in a team can actually help people to feel more motivated in their work as they strive to reach the highest levels of performance and to help one another. This is a benefit for employers and team members equally. Employers get motivated employees, and team members feel motivated by having work that fulfils their needs better than many other jobs.

## The two-factor theory

Frederick Herzberg (an American psychologist and professor) also believed that people had different levels of needs, and that the higher levels would not have any effect unless the lower levels were satisfied. He created just two categories:

- hygiene factors
- motivating factors.

### Hygiene factors
You can think of Herzberg's hygiene factors as being like good personal hygiene. Hygiene does not cure illness, but it can prevent people getting ill in the first place. The factors include pay, relationships at work, working conditions, leadership styles, levels of supervision, security, working hours and status. Herzberg said that the lower-level hygiene factors were necessary, but did not in themselves motivate people. Without them, however, people would be *demotivated*.

### Motivating factors
To really motivate people to work to their full ability Herzberg said they needed to experience motivating factors such as a sense of achievement, responsibility, recognition, promotion possibilities and challenge.

## Similarities

As you can see, many of Herzberg's hygiene factors are like Maslow's middle-level needs. Herzberg's motivating factors are like Maslow's middle and higher-level

> Many features of being in a team, such as a sense of belonging and being respected for your contribution, are important in motivating people.

needs. Herzberg did not concern himself with Maslow's lowest-level needs, which were not a problem for people working in American businesses in the second half of the twentieth century.

## Herzberg's model at work

Herzberg's theories confirm that people who work in teams and have some control over their working lives are likely to be better motivated than those who do not. How you behave as a team leader can have a direct effect on team members. Unless your leadership is supportive and helps to foster good relationships in the team (hygiene factors), then nothing else that is done is likely to motivate people.

# Rewards and motivation

Many people say that money is a motivator. If people feel poorly treated, including being poorly paid, then nothing else you do will motivate them. But simply paying well does not motivate more. Recognising how well people are doing is far more likely to motivate them if they feel that they are being paid fairly.

'Theory X' managers (see Chapter 4) tend to believe that people are motivated only by pay and will aim to do as little as possible for as much money as they can get. In contrast, 'Theory Y' managers think that people want to do their work well and are keen to have a say in what they do and how they do it. Theory Y managers think that people can be motivated by the work they do, their sense of having achieved something worthwhile, and recognition by their managers and team leaders.

## Effort, performance and reward

You do not have to feel wholly like a 'Theory X' manager to think that pay and rewards are important. Another American academic, Victor Vroom, suggested that people are indeed interested in the link between work and rewards. In particular, he argued that people look at:

- the link between effort and performance – how much effort do I need to succeed?
- the link between performance and rewards – does my reward reflect my success?
- the attractiveness of rewards – are the money and other benefits what I really want?

In Vroom's view, people look at all three elements. Only if all three match their expectations are they going to be fully motivated. Conversely, hard work that is not valued and poorly rewarded will not motivate people at all.

How can this theory help you at work? If you believe that there is a link between how hard people work and their pay, then you need to make sure that the effort people put in does affect outcomes – what is called 'working smarter not harder'. Sometimes a lot of effort is wasted because people work inefficiently or lack the necessary skills. Helping people to 'work smarter' means ensuring that they have the skills and can work in ways that directly raise their performance.

Helping people to 'work smarter' means ensuring that they have the skills and can work in ways that directly raise their performance.

## Ways to motivate your team

What all the research and theories suggest is that there are things you can do to ensure that people are motivated to work to the full limits of their ability. We have already seen some of these, such as:

- ensuring that team relationships are positive and that people feel a sense of belonging to the team

- recognising good performance by praising individuals and the whole team for the work they have done (the positive feedback you learnt about in Chapter 11)

- involving people in decision-making and control over their work so that they feel empowered (perhaps using the delegating style of leadership in Chapter 8)

- encouraging and helping people to develop themselves to achieve what they are capable of.

There are some other steps you can take as well. One is to prevent team members finding their work boring or monotonous by ensuring variation. This can be done by rotating, enlarging or enriching jobs (see box below). As team leader you are likely to have more freedom to rotate jobs and can take this into account when deciding who should do what. Job enlargement and job enrichment may well require support from managers but they can each produce real benefits, not just in motivating staff but in reducing time wasted in passing work from one person to another or waiting for other people to complete their part of the task.

## Creating variety

| | |
|---|---|
| Job rotation | Making sure that people have a chance to undertake different tasks, and that the more enjoyable tasks are shared out equally. |
| Job enlargement | Expanding tasks, by encouraging people to get involved in more aspects of an activity. In some factories machine operators get involved in maintenance. In some offices sales staff get involved in after-sales service. |
| Job enrichment | This is an extension of job enlargement, and includes reducing controls over work and making tasks more complex, with added individual or team responsibility. |

## Understanding

Perhaps the most important thing you can do as team leader is to recognise that team members are all individuals who behave in different ways. Some people may be more interested in money or promotion while others prefer the chance to get involved in team roles. Understanding your team's members is the first step towards creating the conditions that motivate them.

## Summary

- Motivation is the desire to perform well in the things we do.

- Team leaders can encourage or discourage others by the way they perform their own role.

- As team leader you are limited in what you can do about money, work conditions or hours (Herzberg's hygiene factors) but you can do something about how the team members relate to one another, about the degree of freedom people have over their work and their involvement in decisions about what they do.

- You can also look at ways of making their work more interesting and enjoyable, possibly with the support of your manager.

- Several motivation theories suggest that lower levels of need must be satisfied before higher levels can be.

- Money is important, but people are concerned about the relationship between how hard they work, the effect on their performance, the amount of reward and the value to them of the reward.

- Working as part of a team can itself be a motivational factor.

## Review your learning

Look through the various theories of motivation and relate them to your own and your team's behaviour.

- Have you ever noticed a team member lose motivation for work because of problems with their family, housing or security that might well be explained by Maslow's hierarchy of needs?

- Do you feel that your employer has ensured that there are adequate 'hygiene factors' in your team's job roles to stop team members feeling demotivated?

- How well does your employer use motivating factors to encourage you and your team to perform to the best of your ability?

- Do you feel more in tune with the Theory X or Theory Y idea of management? Which aspects of your team members' behaviour make you feel one or the other is a better description of what makes people behave as they do?

- Is the link between effort and performance, between performance and reward, and the level of reward sufficiently strong to make you feel motivated?

# 15 | Developing team members' skills

## Introduction

Team leaders can play an active role in ensuring that everybody is encouraged to develop their skills to the highest possible level. This chapter outlines ways to identify the skills that team members need, the skills that team members already possess and the ways in which those skills can be developed. You will also see how you can help others by setting the good example of developing your own skills as a trainer and coach.

## Which skills?

There are many types of skill, ranging across every industry. However, it is possible to distinguish three main types:

- mental skills – for thinking and analysing information; using knowledge; understanding how products, services and equipment operate; working out how to do things

- judgement skills – the skills you use to relate well to people; communicate with them and understand their feelings; and to make judgements about right or wrong, good or bad

- physical skills – for using, making or repairing something, using your hands, tools and other equipment.

Of course, we often use all three types of skill simultaneously. For example, a team member who writes a letter to a customer, replying to a justified complaint, uses mental skills to explain why the problem occurred; judgement skills to apologise for the obvious upset; and physical skills to key in the words quickly and accurately on the computer keyboard. What is needed is to employ all three types of skill well. This is what is called 'being competent'.

## Developing competence

Competence is the ability to perform tasks to the standard required at work. In high-performing teams that standard is a high one, so competent team members can perform to high standards. Competence also involves achieving the required standard without having to struggle. In fact, competence often involves people being able to do something almost without thinking about it.

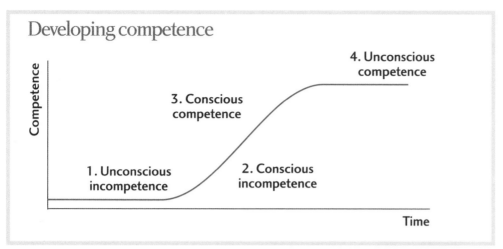

## Developing competence

As the diagram shows, we go through four stages as we develop our competence.

1. Unconscious incompetence – people start by not being aware of what they cannot do, because they have no experience of it at all.

2. Conscious incompetence – as they start to learn how to do it, they realise how difficult it is.

3. Conscious competence – when they acquire skills, they begin to perform competently, so long as they concentrate on what they are doing.

4. Unconscious competence – eventually they can perform competently without even seeming to have to think about it.

When people reach the fourth stage, their competence stops developing. It may even decline if corners get cut or people do not keep up with changes. So, team leaders must not overlook the updating and development needs of experienced team members.

## Which standards?

What are the standards you need to use when you consider whether team members' skills match up to them? The full answer depends on your work, industrial sector and organisation.

Some qualifications are based on national occupational standards which describe what people should be able to do in a job and can be used for defining the competence needed to perform a particular job. You might come across these standards in the form of National Vocational Qualifications (NVQs) and Scottish Vocational Qualifications (SVQs), for example.

Many employers have also developed their own standards of competence for particular jobs. There are also standards of competence that are not written down but are expected of people performing particular tasks. These may be the 'norms' that team members work to. In high-performing teams these are high standards which are consistently observed by team members. A real commitment to high standards of competence means that someone does a job correctly even when nobody else can see or would ever know if they did it poorly or not at all.

# Identifying the skills needed

Before you can identify the skills someone needs to develop, you must establish which skill and competence standards are required for a particular task or job role. You can then assess people against these skill or competence standards. The difference between the skills they need and the skills they have is sometimes called their skills gap. The skills shortages that this shows up can then be put into order of priority for development and that produces the development goals for that person.

You can assess someone in three main ways – by:

- asking them (self-assessment)
- observing them perform the task
- using tests.

Self-assessment is the easiest: it can be useful for fairly straightforward skills where the standard is clear. Observation is often the best way, but can be expensive because it means you are not getting on with the rest of your job. However, it is useful for assessing the most important skills. Tests can be useful for assessing less common skills, or those where there is a risk of injury or damage involved if someone is allowed to perform a task before they have shown that they are competent.

## Using a skills matrix

If you know which skills are needed for each task that your team performs, you can create a skills matrix. This is a table showing the tasks, skills and the team members. You can decide who is likely to undertake each task and whether or not they are already competent to do this. If they are not competent, you can identify the training and development they need. There is an example of a skills matrix in the box below. You can include in your skills matrix the dates when people will start training or expect to be trained. Other columns could show qualifications, such as the ILM Team Leader Certificate, or standard in-house training activities.

## An excerpt from a skills matrix

| Task | Serve customers | | Service mowers | | |
|------|------------------|------------------|------------------|------------------|------------------|
| Skills | Product knowledge | Customer service | Petrol motors | Hand mowers | Ride-on mowers |
| Orla Smith | C | C | T | W | W |
| Dan Mo | C | C | C | C | T |

C = Competent
T = Being trained
W = Waiting to be trained

# Training and coaching

As team leader, you may be expected to organise ways to help team members to develop their skills, or to train or coach them yourself. (In *Leading Teams* we use the word 'training' to mean only the formal training of groups of people. In contrast, we use 'coaching' to indicate a way of developing individuals on a one-to-one basis.) However, you may first need to discuss with your employer your own training and development as a trainer or coach.

## Training

Formal training is often used to develop team members' knowledge and understanding of products, services, processes or procedures or to learn how to do things. Formal training sessions are often organised away from the workplace. If, however, they are run in-house, people should not be expected to do their normal work tasks. If you are asked to train your team, you might find it helpful to work through the following steps.

Step 1: Have clear objectives. These should say what the *trainees* will be able to do by the end of the training, not what you will be doing as the trainer.

Step 2: Find out what the trainees already know and can do. Always start the training from where people are and build on that. By reminding people what they can *already* do, you can then make them aware of what they need to learn.

Step 3: Break what they need to learn into its simplest parts. For example, if you are explaining how to use a new item of equipment, include the various parts, its uses and the actions that the users can take.

Step 4: Work out the best order to cover each of these parts. Sometimes this will be obvious – such as switching on a machine – but you might have to make a decision based on what the learners need to learn.

Step 5: Prepare thoroughly. The best routine for the training session is:

- tell the trainees how to do it – to introduce the trainees to the topic or practice

- show the trainees how to do it – so they see what they have to do

- let the trainees do it – this is how many people really learn best.

Learners might be able to practise in the workplace with the actual equipment, but a simulation may be just as helpful because people are safe to make mistakes and to learn from them without causing any harm. This will help them to develop their conscious competence.

Step 6: Review what you have covered and what they have learnt. Ask plenty of questions to check their learning and, if it is appropriate, test them, using the training objectives as the standard for your judgement. Above all, make sure that the learners feel confident to carry out what they have just learnt and are ready to do so. In time, they will move from conscious competence to unconscious competence.

> A real commitment to high standards of competence means that someone does a job correctly even when nobody else can see or would ever know if they did it poorly or not at all.

*Training aids*

Make sure that you have all the necessary facilities, equipment and training aids ready for the training session – and make sure you can use them. These could include rooms, workshops or other facilities; equipment, products and materials; notes, handouts and manuals; and visual aids, such as a wall diagram, picture, video, overhead projector (OHP) acetates or a computer-based presentation. When using text on visual aids, use single words or short phrases, as in the example below.

---

## Food slicer safety

- Switch off before loading

- Check guard is in place

- Use only for cooked meats

- Use metal protection plate to push meat onto blade

---

## Coaching

Coaching is a type of informal, one-to-one training in the workplace. It is an effective way of developing individual performance and is particularly useful with new team members who need to learn how to do a specific task or use a specific piece of equipment.

The disadvantage of coaching is that it is an expensive way of developing someone, as the coach helps only one person at a time. However, it is usually quicker for the person being coached, compared to being part of a group. In fact, the best way is to train people in the basics, then coach them to the highest standards of performance you can, helping them to move from conscious to unconscious competence.

The coaching steps are similar to those for training, the only difference being step five.

Step 1:   Have clear objectives.

Step 2:   Find out what the trainees already know and can do.

Step 3:   Break what they need to learn into its simplest parts.

Step 4:   Work out the best order to cover each of these parts.

Step 5:   Encourage the trainee to try out the tasks and ask them questions such as:

- what do you think is the first step?

- which of these options do you think is the right one?

- what do you think will happen if you do that?

Step 6:   Review what you have covered and what the person being coached has learnt.

When coaching, resist the temptation to tell people what to do or, even worse, show them, unless it is really necessary. What people work out for themselves, they remember best. Your role is to ensure that what they remember and practise is correct.

## Leading by example

As a team leader, you are responsible for ensuring that team members have the skills they need to perform to the highest standards. This includes accepting responsibility for your own development, as you saw in Chapter 8. High-performing teams need high-performing team leaders, so seize every opportunity to learn and improve your own knowledge and skills. Lead by example: if you take your own development seriously, then other members of your team will appreciate that it is important.'

## Summary

- Competence is the ability to perform a task to the standard required.

- Most tasks require a combination of different types of skill, including thinking, analysing and using knowledge and understanding; relating well to people, communicating and understanding feelings; and making or doing things, using your hands, tools and other equipment.

- Before people learn anything their skills should be assessed by self-assessment, observation or testing. A skills matrix can be used to compare the skills people have with what they need.

- Team leaders should be able to train and coach team members, following a six-step process.

## Review your learning

Look back at any training or coaching that you have organised or received.

- How were the six steps followed? If they were not followed, would the six steps have improved the training or coaching, and how?

- Which training or coaching aids were used? Were they prepared in advance? How effective were they?

- Did you see or experience the four stages in developing competence, from unconscious incompetence to unconscious competence?

- What worked best in the training or coaching?

- What most needed to be improved?

> What people work out for themselves, they remember best. Your role is to ensure that what they remember and practise is correct.

# 16 | Everyone is different

## Introduction

There is more to a team than just having people who can do a job well. Team members must also be prepared to work together, support one another and ensure that the team meets its goals. To do so, team members need to have respect for one another and to value the contribution that each person can make. This chapter looks at how team members treat one another and anyone else they meet in the course of their work.

## Diversity matters

People come from a great variety of backgrounds and everyone is different. This is described as diversity. But, whatever their differences, everyone has the right to be treated fairly and equally. Such rights are backed up by laws that make it illegal to put up artificial barriers to people's work opportunities and treatment. It is against the law, for example, to exclude people from jobs because they are married or have a particular skin colour. Employers are also obliged to make the workplace accessible for people who have often previously been excluded, such as those with impaired sight, hearing or mobility.

People must be appointed to jobs because of their ability, or their potential ability, and not because of any 'difference' that plays no part in their ability to do the job. What's more, it is good practice to reflect the diversity of a community in the workplace and in individual teams.

Diversity is not only about making concerted efforts to tolerate people's differences, and not discriminate against them. It is, more importantly, about inclusivity – making an effort to ensure that *everyone* is included in all aspects of the team's activities.

Your role is to take a lead in actively including people by, for example, encouraging everyone to play an equal part and ensuring that the existing team does not create barriers for others.

## Prejudice

Even so, prejudice – an unfavourable, or hostile, opinion formed before knowledge or experience of something – still exists in society in general and in the workplace. Some people are excluded or passed over for opportunities or promotion despite their ability. As a team leader, you must ensure that everyone in your team behaves in ways that make opportunities equal, fair and legal.

# Discrimination

Discrimination means unfair or unequal treatment or opportunities. It is illegal to unfairly exclude someone from jobs, training or promotion on the grounds of their:

- sex
- racial or ethnic origin
- sexual orientation
- religion or belief
- disability
- age.

Anyone who believes that they have experienced discriminatory behaviour and suffered as a consequence has a legal right to make a complaint and to apply for compensation at an Employment Tribunal.

## Discrimination at work

Discrimination at work occurs in two ways. Direct discrimination occurs when an employer makes decisions on the basis of someone's sex, race or some other factor that has no bearing on their ability to do something.

Indirect discrimination occurs when conditions are imposed that are not relevant to the job and make it difficult for, or exclude, certain groups or individuals. For example, a requirement for someone to be able to lift heavy weights in a job that involves moving only a few sheets of paper at a time discriminates against some people. The only conditions that can be made are those that are a specific requirement of the job.

It is not difficult to keep within the law. Just remember that people should be selected for a job, a task or for training only on the basis of:

- the requirements of the job
- the person's ability to meet these requirements.

You may not be responsible for recruiting or promoting people or for deciding who goes on training courses, but you may be asked by your manager for your help and advice. If what you say could lead the organisation to do something discriminatory, it could end up in court. Ignorance of the law, or unintentional discrimination, is not an excuse.

## Keeping the law

In Chapter 15 you saw how you can look at tasks to see which skills are needed. If you are asked what kind of person you need to fill a vacancy in your team, start off by saying which tasks the person will need to do, and the skills they will need to perform them. For example, the tasks and skills required to work in a warehouse in the UK may include:

- driving a forklift truck
- stacking and picking goods stored on pallets
- reading labels and recording goods in and out of stock
- using a computer to enter and extract information.

The jobholder does not need to be physically strong, as all the heavy work is mechanised. A basic knowledge of English is needed for reading the details and instructions on delivery and picking notes, but not a high level of proficiency in written or spoken English. The person could be trained to use the particular computer software, so the jobholder may need only basic computing skills.

Even so, many organisations still employ only men to drive forklift trucks. They assume that moving heavy items needs physical strength and that women do not have that strength.

Some organisations find reasons not to employ someone who is not able to walk, although they could spend the whole day sitting down. Others turn away someone who speaks English as a second language, although they can read and write well enough to do the job competently.

This is discriminatory, which is illegal, and short-sighted. It is discriminatory because it excludes people without a valid legal reason. It is short-sighted because it excludes people who may do the job as well or better than those currently doing it.

What's more, there are grants available to help organisations to obtain special equipment, such as Braille keyboards or software that converts text on a computer screen to speech, to enable people to do jobs where there have previously been barriers to that employment.

*Exceptions*
There are only a few jobs where the law allows restrictions on who is appointed on the basis of discrimination – an employer can, for example, insist that an attendant in a women's changing room is a female employee.

## Discriminatory behaviour

Discrimination does not always occur because of decisions that are made when recruiting or training people. It often happens because the behaviour of people in the workplace actively discourages individuals from working there, or it makes life so uncomfortable that they feel harassed.

Harassment means that someone's life is made miserable by the repeated, unwelcome or hostile actions of other people.

As a team leader, it is your responsibility to take action if any of your team members' actions could be seen as being discriminatory or potentially discriminatory towards other team members or anyone else the team members have contact with as part of their work. It is no excuse to say such things as, "Oh they are always like that. They don't mean any harm." It does not matter how long the behaviour has been going on, or what they intended the outcome to be. It is still a problem.

Inclusivity involves making an effort to ensure that everyone is included in all aspects of the team's activities.

## A discriminatory workplace culture

Culture has been defined as 'how things are done around here'. If things are done in a way that discriminates against people or harasses them in any way, then you have the wrong kind of culture. Examples of inappropriate behaviour that could indicate a discriminatory culture are shown in the box below. A team cannot work at its best if there is any discriminatory behaviour or harassment towards team members or people outside the team. It will affect a team member's performance, or discourage a customer or supplier from doing further business with your organisation. Worst of all, it shows a lack of respect for others, and a team without respect for others can never expect any respect itself.

Although women and people who are part of a minority in society are the main sufferers from discriminatory or harassing behaviour at work, anybody can be in a minority in the workplace and suffer discrimination or harassment. Young men working in largely female work environments have successfully complained about sexual harassment after being made fun of constantly. Nobody should feel that they are being discriminated against or being harassed at work.

| Behaviour | Examples |
|---|---|
| The use of offensive or discriminatory language, including the use of obscenities. This includes ways of speaking that are condescending, rude or belittling. | "You don't want that size, darling. That's man-sized." (Obscenities, or strong language, offend many people. There is no reason why they should be used in the workplace.) |
| Nicknames that are based on personal characteristics. | Calling a Muslim 'Ayatollah' or a person with a limp 'Hopalong'. |
| Displaying signs, pictures or other materials that are likely to offend. | Pin-up calendars and soft-porn magazines. |

## Bullying at work

Bullying is the description given to some discriminatory behaviour that is directed at a particular individual rather than at a group of people. It ranges from constant derogatory comments, abusive remarks and behaviour that make someone's life miserable, to intimidating behaviour, including physical violence. Bullying is always unpleasant but at its worst can cause people to suffer from clinical depression and even to commit suicide. Bullying makes the bully feel more powerful, but makes the target of the bullying feel powerless. Many bullies bully others to make themselves feel better. A team will always be weakened by having members who do not show respect for other team members. It is the bully who makes the team weaker, although the effect may be in the performance of the person being bullied.

## Challenging discriminatory behaviour

You need to be prepared to act if you believe that the behaviour of any member of your team is likely to be regarded as offensive, discriminatory, harassing or bullying.

However, if someone *complains* about such behaviour, you should not try to deal with it yourself, unless the complainant has specifically asked *you* to say something to the person responsible. Unless that is the case, you should always report it to your manager as soon as possible. Ideally, write a note of what happened so that you have a written record of the event. This could be helpful later, especially if the problem finishes up in an employment tribunal or a court.

You should also make a report to your manager even when no complaint has been made if you believe the behaviour is severe enough for some sort of disciplinary action to be needed. This will be the case if *you* saw behaviour that was clearly offensive, discriminatory, harassing or bullying. If you do nothing it will certainly encourage the offender to believe that the behaviour is acceptable.

If the behaviour is mild or appears to be unintentional, you should still take action. You may not want to make it into a formal disciplinary matter, but that does not stop you from doing something about it yourself. Speak to the person or people involved, in private. Tell them what you saw or heard, not what you think about them and their intentions. (You don't know why they did it.) Point out that their behaviour could cause offence and may be illegal. If a complaint were to be made they could lose their job. Emphasise that it does not matter what they *intended*, it is the *effect* that matters. Do not make it personal or lose your temper. The next chapter deals with conflict or potential conflict at work, and applies here too.

## A team leader's responsibility

A team leader has very little power, although a great deal of responsibility and influence. It is very difficult to make people do something by threatening them when you do not have the power to do much if the threat does not work. In any case, threats are rarely the best way to get people to change their behaviour. As a team leader you can only:

- set a good example, showing people what you expect from them

- encourage the team members to respect one another, and emphasise that anything that affects one member affects the whole team in one way or another

- be prepared to take action as soon as something happens, to try to stop it before it gets serious.

### Leading with respect

Always remember that discrimination, harassment and bullying are not just illegal, they are very unpleasant things to experience. The person who is on the receiving end is being made to suffer for simply being who they are. You would not want to suffer the same sort of behaviour and should not allow it to happen to anybody else. Welcome the chance to learn about people who are different from other team members, and treat everyone as you would want them to treat you.

> As a team leader, you must ensure that everyone in your team behaves in ways that make opportunities equal, fair and legal.

# Summary

- Discrimination against people on the basis of their sex, racial or ethnic origin, sexual orientation, religion or belief, disability or age is illegal and employers can suffer heavy financial penalties for allowing it to happen.

- Discrimination can be direct (explicitly discriminating against a group of people) or indirect (making conditions that are not required by the job but which have the effect of discriminating against a particular group).

- Bullying is directed at individuals rather than groups. It ranges from constant derogatory behaviour or abuse to physical aggression.

- Always make decisions about people on the basis of the requirements of the job and their ability to meet these requirements.

- You are responsible for creating a team culture in which team members do not accept discriminatory, offensive, harassing or bullying language or behaviour.

- A team leader should always be prepared to challenge behaviour or language that may be offensive, discriminatory, harassing or bullying. Always say what you see and hear, not what you think is causing the person to behave like that. Keep a record of what you have done.

- A team leader should set a good example, encourage team members to respect one another and, if necessary, be prepared to take action.

- Aim for inclusivity, not discrimination.

# Review your learning

Look at your team and consider the following questions.

- Does its membership reasonably reflect the society in which you live? Remember that communities vary around the country, and your team should aim to reflect local diversity.

- Could any of the behaviour or language of your team members be interpreted as offensive, discriminatory, harassing or bullying to team members, other team members, customers or suppliers?

- Do you set a good example when it comes to encouraging your team to be open and welcoming to the diversity of the society in which they live?

- What could your team do to improve its inclusivity?

# 17 | Handling conflict

## Introduction

The members of high-performing teams often disagree among themselves. This can have a positive effect if it generates new ideas and prompts improvements in how the team works. However, disagreements that are not resolved can lead to conflict, with long-term, damaging consequences.

This chapter outlines the main sources of conflict, clues to recognising it and ways of dealing with it. You will also read about the three main personal styles that you can adopt to prevent or deal with conflict, the function of disciplinary procedures and your role in ensuring that any disciplinary action is fair.

## Disagreement and conflict

Disagreement is a natural part of living and working with other people, because people have their own ideas and opinions and can feel strongly about things.

Although harmony at work is positive, occasional *disagreement* can indicate that there is active debate and discussion, which is not always bad. Indeed, if you do not see or hear any disagreement, then you may need to be more alert to it, or it may be that the team is drifting along and avoiding conflict by not trying hard enough.

Conflict can, however, result from strong disagreements that remain unresolved. In the worst cases, comments can become heated and behaviour can become violent. Even a minor conflict can create tension that disrupts work, creates animosity and reduces the team's effectiveness.

### Healthy debate

Effective team leaders encourage discussion and decision-making. There are often differences of opinion about what to do, how to do it or the consequences of doing something. There may also be differences in people's values or beliefs.

Disagreement and even some conflict can result from tension as people become familiar with new ways of working and work out the details of the change, or when there are non-routine tasks to tackle. People argue strongly for their preferred solution, as part of the process of finding new ways of doing things. But by sharing their thoughts in a co-operative atmosphere, people learn and develop new ideas. From this often comes new understanding and a commitment to new ways of working, which, in turn, leads to greater team cohesion or a sense of belonging.

## The sources and dangers of conflict

Conflict often arises when team members do not share goals. This tends to happen when:

- there is competition among team members for power or benefits
- individuals pursue personal goals at the expense of team goals
- there is a lack of control in the team, with the result that people follow their own goals
- personal grudges and animosity occur, possibly arising from discriminatory, harassing or bullying behaviour or language, or from personality clashes
- there is poor communication between team members, leading to a lack of understanding or awareness.

As a general rule, conflicts relating to routine tasks (the ones performed regularly and in the same way) have harmful consequences that reduce team effectiveness. Such conflicts often arise out of boredom, monotony and a lack of any sense of achievement. Conflicts relating to relationships can also be harmful. They tend to be emotional and are among the most difficult to resolve.

*Weakening the team*
Conflict usually leads to problems or poor relationships and a weakening of the team. The specific problems include:

- stress and ill feeling between team members
- poor communication (people not talking to each other)
- a lack of focus on the team's goals
- poor or slow decision-making as people become reluctant to agree with other team members.

## Setting an example

The symptoms of conflict (what you see and hear) may not be the causes (why people are in conflict). Competition between team members, for example, could stem from your own behaviour as team leader in playing members off one against another, or seeming to favour one person and then another. Although the team might seem over-competitive, your leadership style (see Chapter 8) could be inappropriate, or you could lack confidence in your role.

## Personal style

Before you can learn how to resolve conflict you need to have some insight into the three main personal styles that people adopt when facing conflict:

- aggressive
- passive
- assertive.

> Although harmony at work is positive, occasional *disagreement* can indicate that there is active debate and discussion, which is not always bad.

## Aggressive behaviour

Aggressive behaviour reveals what people are thinking or feeling, or what they believe, in a manner that is likely to humiliate another person or make them feel weak or powerless. Aggressive people show little respect for the needs or feelings of others. Aggressive behaviour may be merely verbal, but it can become intimidating or threatening. Once an aggressive style becomes a violent one, then the matter is a disciplinary issue, and not one that you should attempt to deal with.

## Passive behaviour

Passive behaviour is when people hide what they are really thinking and feeling, or what they believe. They may simply accept what other people say or do. Alternatively, they may be so apologetic, diffident or self-effacing in expressing themselves that nobody listens to them. Conflict often occurs when aggressive people disagree. But it also happens when aggressive people challenge passive people. Some aggressive people keep on at passive people to see if they can get them to become aggressive.

## Assertive behaviour

Assertiveness is not the midpoint between the two, a mixture of aggression and passivity. Instead, think of it as the third point in a triangle. It is an *alternative* style. Assertive behaviour means saying what you are thinking or feeling and what you believe directly and honestly, without challenging or disapproving of others. Assertive people show respect for their own needs and feelings as well as the needs and feelings of the other person. To help you to develop an assertive style, there are ten points you should remember

## Ten points to assertiveness

1. Be clear about your own thoughts, feelings and values.

2. Ask questions so you know what it is you are expected to comment on.

3. Take time to think before you say what you mean. Do not let yourself be rushed into agreeing with others.

4. Do not attempt to over-justify your own views. Be brief and succinct about what you think, feel or believe so that people cannot try to argue with every detail.

5. Say "no" when you mean 'no' and try, "I've decided not to" instead of, "I can't". It is your choice not to do something.

6. Let your body language confirm your words, do not avoid people's gaze as if you are ashamed of making your own decision.

7. If your decision is ignored or challenged, repeat it, but do not attempt to justify it again. Do not allow the conversation to persist if the other person will not accept your decision.

8. Look for a compromise position (if there is one) that still meets other people's major concerns but also produces the outcome you want.

9. Acknowledge any disappointment at your decision ("I realise you won't like this, …") but do not apologise unless there is a very good reason for doing so. You do not have to do what anybody else wants, or feel guilty about it.

10. Acknowledge that you were wrong if your decision has not worked as you intended. Be willing to accept an alternative you previously rejected.

Assertiveness does not stop conflict, but it can help to reduce it by easing some of the emotion that makes conflict so destructive.

### Assertiveness and co-operation

Teams are built on co-operation, mutual help and support for team members. Co-operation puts the team before self. But assertiveness is largely about yourself and about achieving what *you* want. So, how can there be effective teams with assertive people in them? But without them, how would the team survive and thrive?

In practice, teams full of assertive people can become aggressive at times, if they really care about the subject. Alternatively, they become rather passive if they are not too bothered. In high-performing teams the members recognise that they need to balance their assertiveness with the need to co-operate with the rest of the team.

Encourage your team members to be assertive and yet, at the same time, to co-operate. Set a good example yourself. Demonstrate how you can be assertive without being aggressive, co-operate without being passive. Look for the outcome that ensures that everyone gets the best out of the deal.

The box below shows how different personal styles can affect the team's performance.

## Teams and personal styles

| If each member of the team were: | The team would be: |
| --- | --- |
| Aggressive | Full of conflict with members trying to force their ideas down the others' throats, leading to verbal and even physical fights. |
| Passive | Ineffective, because nobody wants to take the lead or make decisions. The least passive person reluctantly leads the others, but fairly aimlessly. |
| Assertive | Full of ideas, willing to listen to others and respect their point of view, but wanting the same treatment. Plenty of ideas will be put forward and compromises will be made only if everyone feels that they are achieving what they regard as most important in the outcome. |

# Handling conflict

Assertiveness is important if you have to deal with conflicts, especially long-standing ones. Being assertive includes facing up to situations, not ignoring them and hoping they will go away. Here are five steps to help you to resolve conflict.

Step 1: Find out the facts. Ask each person for his or her account of the problem, away from the scene of any conflict if possible. Just listen to your colleagues' accounts and avoid making judgements or putting another point of view. Try to separate the people from the problem, by focussing on facts rather than opinions, or feelings.

Step 2: Review what has been said, identify common ground and what is most important for all those involved (their priorities).

Step 3: Present your conclusions to each in turn, starting with the common ground and getting agreement to those points (in turn) and to the order of priority.

Step 4: Look for the solution that will enable the warring parties to get as much of what they each want, if you believe that this is a reasonable and appropriate outcome. This gives each party a partial 'win'. Alternatively, look for a solution that is radically different to those they have already considered, but which meets all or most of their concerns.

Step 5: If neither of the outcomes outlined in Step 4 is possible, make the decision that you feel is best for the team as a whole, rather than for any individual. If one person is perceived to have 'lost', acknowledge it and say that it was for the benefit of the team as a whole, not the 'winner' in the conflict. Do not be afraid to assert your right to make a decision if the parties cannot agree.

## If the problem will not go away...

Sometimes it is impossible to resolve a conflict satisfactorily. This can happen if it has become so personal that it has caused a complete breakdown between the individuals involved. If the conflict has led to any violence, physical intimidation, threats against you or other team members or the undermining of the team or its work, then you need to treat it as a disciplinary issue.

# Discipline at work

Disagreement and even minor conflict at work is often healthy and productive, and it is not necessarily a disciplinary issue. Discipline is the enforcing of the rules of the organisation that employees are expected to observe. The rules are usually set out in policies and procedures, covering such issues as:

- health and safety and environmental protection, to ensure that team members and others are not at risk of harm

- equality of opportunity and diversity at work, to ensure that people are treated fairly and legally

- privacy, confidentiality and security, to ensure that products, services, information and resources (including money) are not misused

- general behaviour and responsibilities, such as timekeeping, absence from work and performance at work.

If someone fails to keep to the rules, make it clear that they will be disciplined. Most organisations have a clear disciplinary policy that they have drawn up themselves or is based on a standard policy available from the Advisory, Conciliation and Arbitration Service (ACAS), a UK government-funded service.

Before taking any disciplinary steps an employer must investigate and give the person a chance to explain their behaviour.

Team leaders are not normally expected to deal with breaches of discipline themselves, but are likely to be a witness and can be questioned by the manager investigating the situation and by the team member involved. This is why you should record any action you have taken in a conflict or if someone has been behaving in a way that offends, discriminates against, harasses or bullies others.

## Disciplinary action

There are usually three steps in taking disciplinary action.

1. First warning. This is usually an *oral* (face-to-face) warning by the line manager that the behaviour will not be tolerated. The person should be told that a note will be kept of the warning for a specific period, usually six months. If the offence is more serious, a first formal *written* warning may be given and stay in effect for longer, perhaps 12 months.

2. Final (written) warning. If the behaviour does not improve, then a second warning should be given. This must be a *written* warning. The person should be told that they face dismissal or some other sanction (for example, being demoted) if they repeat the misconduct or do not improve performance. It is possible to give a *final* written warning *without* a first warning if the behaviour is very serious but does not warrant dismissal.

3. Dismissal, demotion or other 'punishment'. This is done if the behaviour that the person has been warned about is repeated. It usually involves being given one or two weeks' notice of dismissal, or money in place of notice. If the behaviour is regarded as gross misconduct (for example, physical violence or stealing), then the person may be dismissed without notice and without prior warning. Conflict at work could lead to gross misconduct, which is why you should take action to prevent it from escalating as soon as you spot any symptoms.

A disciplinary hearing is not a pleasant experience but it is one of the responsibilities involved in being a team leader. Do not say what you believe other people were thinking or feeling, just what you saw, thought or felt yourself. You will not be making any decisions but simply describing what happened.

In the long run, disciplinary action will ensure that the team is able to perform better than it would otherwise do, and that is the one benefit of the process.

Record any action you have taken in a conflict or if someone has been behaving in a way that offends, discriminates against, harasses or bullies others.

## Summary

- Conflict is a possible consequence of unresolved disagreements.

- Conflict can be healthy if it arises through disagreements over how to move forward, but is unhealthy if it arises from competition between people, personal ambition or animosity, or poor control or communications.

- You and your team members' personal styles can cause or deter conflict. The three main styles people adopt are aggressive, passive and assertive, of which only the assertive style is productive.

- For teams to be effective, assertiveness needs to be balanced by a willingness of team members to co-operate, so that they balance their own individual needs with the needs of the team as a whole.

- You can help to resolve conflicts between team members by:

  1. Finding out the facts

  2. Identifying common ground and priorities

  3. Presenting your conclusions and getting team members' agreement

  4. Finding a compromise that gives each person a partial 'win', or proposing something radically different

  5. If neither a compromise nor a radically different solution is possible, make the decision that you feel is best for the team as a whole.

- Disciplinary action is taken if people fail to obey the rules of the organisation.

- A team leader does not usually take disciplinary action but may give evidence to an investigation.

- A team member being disciplined may receive a first oral warning, a final written warning and then dismissal or other sanction. If the offence is very serious (such as violence or theft) the employee may be sacked immediately for gross misconduct.

> Disagreements that are not resolved can lead to conflict, with long-term, damaging consequences.

## Review your learning

Assess your own personal style. Are you assertive enough at work? Could you be more assertive to ensure that the team works more effectively, or does your assertiveness sometimes come over as aggressiveness?

Use the ten points to assertiveness (see pages 104-105) to help you to develop your assertive style whilst balancing it with an emphasis on co-operation in the team.

# Working towards quality

Unless team members work safely, efficiently and effectively, then the organisation will suffer. Team leaders work as part of their teams, so they are best placed to ensure that work practices conform to the standards set for the team.

This section looks at how teams can ensure that the goods and services the organisation provides meet the requirements of the people for whom they are provided. It concentrates on what team leaders can do to ensure that their teams do work safely, securely, efficiently and effectively to achieve their goals.

Ensuring a healthy and safe environment for the team is probably the most significant role that team leaders have. Without such conditions, every other goal becomes redundant.

The range of resources and the effect that their use has on the organisation's costs are explained, together with some of the steps that team leaders can take to ensure that the team's resources are used as effectively as possible and that costs are kept under control. This section also shows you some of the techniques available for identifying the source of problems in the production of goods and the supply of services, and how to take the lead in ensuring continuous improvement.

Team working has been developed in all types of organisation as a means of improving quality. As a team leader, you are the key to ensuring that your team performs to the highest standards and helps your organisation to achieve its goals.

# 18 | Safety – the main priority

## Introduction

Ensuring that people are not injured or killed, and that your team does not endanger future generations are, without doubt, the most serious of your responsibilities as a team leader. In this chapter you will learn about the difference between hazards and risks, what you can do to reduce hazards or risks at work, and what you should do if things go wrong. You will also learn about some of the most important legal requirements that affect your work.

## Hazards and risks

What do an electricity socket, a flight of stairs and a delivery vehicle have in common? They are all workplace hazards. Someone could get an electric shock from the socket, fall down a flight of stairs or be knocked over by a vehicle. Of course, if the organisation has a well maintained electric system, has non-slip surfaces on stairs, has secure handrails alongside, keeps its stairways clear and clean, and vehicles are driven carefully and are well maintained, then the risk that an accident will occur is very low.

As you can see, a hazard is any activity, equipment or circumstance that could cause harm or injury. Risk is the chance that it might happen. Hazards cause accidents: risks are the likelihood that an accident will happen.

Hazards exist everywhere, but the risk of getting killed at work is really quite low. The death rate is just over 1 in 100,000 (0.001%), although this still means that up to 300 people die in their workplace every year in the UK. The chance of a serious injury is much higher, with about 27,000 people a year losing limbs, breaking bones or losing their eyesight. Of course, some workplaces are far more dangerous than others. Quarries, mines, farms and building sites head the list, along with timber yards and some factories, for the numbers killed and injured.

### The most common causes of workplace accidents

- Falling from heights, such as ladders, scaffolding or roofs.
- Being hit or caught by a moving object, such as a vehicle or a piece of machinery.
- Being hit by something falling from a height, such as materials coming down a chute or equipment dropped by someone working above.

## Other causes of workplace accidents

- Slipping on wet or greasy surfaces or tripping over objects such as trailing cables.

- Cuts from blades, sharp surfaces and edges.

- Electric shocks.

- Burns from hot objects or fire.

- Chemical 'burns', poisoning and other harm from substances (such as cleaning chemicals or pesticides).

- Injury as a result of violence from others (a particular risk for police officers and door stewards, for example).

# Preventing accidents

Many accidents at work happen because:

- hazards exist but are not taken seriously

- the way people behave increases the risk of death or injury.

The existence of a hazard does not, in itself, make it risky. It is possible to take such care around the hazard that there is little or no risk. On the other hand, a workplace may have very few hazards but the way people behave makes it a very risky place to be.

## Identifying hazards

To reduce the risk to health and safety at work, the law requires organisations to carry out risk assessments. The first step is to identify every hazard. These might include trailing electric cables, unlabelled containers of chemicals, unsecured ladders, filing cabinet drawers left open or stock piled in tall stacks, for example.

The best way to reduce the risk of injury or damage is to get rid of the hazard. This could mean banning vehicles from a site, for example. As team leader, you should be aware of all the significant hazards that exist in your workplace and look for practical ways of getting rid of any of them.

## Assessing risks

Even so, not all hazards can be eliminated, so there have to be judgements about the level of risk associated with a hazard to decide what, if anything, needs to be done. Scissors are hazardous but the risk is small unless they are used recklessly or in the wrong way. It's common practice to classify risk as one of three categories:

- high risk

- medium risk

- low risk.

High risks arise when there is a strong chance of there being an accident from a hazard, or the accident could be very serious. Medium-risk hazards are less likely to cause accidents, or are likely to have less serious consequences. Low risks are unlikely to happen or will cause only a minor accident.

Although the judgement of risk may be straightforward in many cases, it is good practice to ensure that team leaders, supervisors and others involved in risk assessment receive adequate specialised training. The likelihood of an accident, the severity of the consequences, the vulnerability of particular groups of people exposed to the hazard, and the number exposed are among the issues to be examined for each hazard identified.

## Reducing risks

There are six steps to take to reduce the risk of accidents at work. These six steps, often referred to as a 'hierarchy of control', are in order of importance.

## Hierarchy of control

1. **Remove the hazard.**

2. **Eliminate or reduce the risk**

3. **Guard the hazard.**

4. **Train the operator or user.**

5. **Supervise the operator or user.**

6. **Protect the operator or user with personal protective equipment (PPE).**

Any attempt to improve safety should work through the steps in order. The first step is to try to remove the hazard entirely. If this is not possible, it may be possible to substitute equipment or a way of doing things that is safer – erecting scaffolding rather than using a ladder, for instance. If this does not make the work safe, then it may be possible to introduce other controls nearby – fencing in a vehicle marshalling area, installing guards on machinery or fitting speed limiters on forklift trucks, for example. Changes to the way things are done can help to make work far safer, and it is essential to ensure that the people who operate machines and equipment or use materials are properly trained. They need to know what the hazards are and how to avoid them. If the risk is still great, particularly if the people concerned are new to the role despite being trained, then they should be supervised to ensure their safety. As a last resort, if this sequence of steps, or a combination of safety measures, still leaves people at risk, then they should be issued with the appropriate personal protective equipment (PPE).

*Leading the way*

As a team leader, you should always be aware of any hazards and look for ways to get rid of them. If they cannot be eliminated, ensure that you do everything possible to reduce the risks they present. Keep a close eye on your colleagues' safety and well-being and demonstrate that you observe all the rules about health and safety.

# An employer's legal responsibilities

The main piece of legislation governing health and safety in the workplace in England, Wales and Scotland is the Health and Safety at Work etc. Act 1974. In Northern Ireland there is similar provision under the Health and Safety at Work (Northern Ireland) Order 1978.

The legislation lays down the responsibilities of:

- employers towards their employees
- employers towards members of the public
- employees for their own health and safety and that of others.

Health and safety enforcement is the responsibility of the Health and Safety Executive (HSE) or the local authority (mainly for organisations where food is involved). The enforcement officers can prosecute employers and employees who do not follow the rules set down.

Although the Act (and the Order in Northern Ireland) requires employers and employees to ensure that they work safely, they should do this 'so far as is reasonably practicable'. In other words, an employer cannot be expected to create a workplace where there are no hazards and no risks. However, they should take good care to identify the particular hazards involved in their activities, assess the risks from them and take sensible precautions.

The Act does not state what should be done under every circumstance. Instead, it sets out some general principles which are expanded by the HSE through:

- regulations
- approved codes of practice
- guidance.

> As a team leader, you should always be aware of any hazards and look for ways to get rid of them.

## Regulations

Regulations are made under the Act and lay down specific rules about particular work activities. Regulations have the force of law. Many are worded to comply with European Union (EU) directives and are common across the union. For example, all employers in member states must carry out risk assessments, have appropriate safety measures in place, appoint competent people and inform and train employees.

Some regulations are specific, dealing with, for example, the handling of asbestos or explosives, working with electricity or gas, or working in a noisy environment. Other regulations apply more generally. Those that affect most workplaces are listed over the page.

## Approved Codes of Practice

These have a special legal status, similar to that of the Highway Code. They describe how to perform tasks or activities that have significant health and safety risks. An employer who has not followed the Approved Code of Practice and is prosecuted under the Health and Safety at Work etc. Act (because of a death or serious injury at work) is more likely to be found guilty.

## Guidance

Guidance, usually in the form of HSE leaflets, is designed to help people to perform tasks safely. It tends to relate to particular work sectors or types of activity. You may, for example, have to follow certain procedures (for which you have been trained) when you have to perform certain tasks that have health and safety risks.

### Health and Safety at Work Regulations

| Title | Key points covered |
|---|---|
| Health and Safety (Display Screen Equipment) Regulations 1992 | Working with visual display units (VDUs) – eg. computer monitors. |
| Personal Protective Equipment at Work Regulations 1992 | Employers must provide protective clothing and equipment where appropriate, to minimise risk. |
| Manual Handling Operations Regulations 1992 | How to lift and move heavy objects. |
| Health and Safety (First Aid) Regulations 1981 | Requirements for first aid at work. |
| Reporting of Injuries, Diseases and Dangerous Occurrences Regulations 1995 (known as RIDDOR) | Employers must record and notify the HSE about certain injuries, diseases and dangerous events at work. |
| Control of Substances Hazardous to Health Regulations 2002 (known as COSHH) | Employers must assess the risks from hazardous substances (eg. toxic chemicals) and take appropriate precautions. |
| Chemicals (Hazard Information and Packaging for Supply) Regulations 2002 (known as CHIP) | Suppliers must label and package dangerous chemicals and provide safety data sheets for them. |

## Your responsibility

As a team leader you are expected to know how to perform hazardous tasks correctly, as laid down in any HSE guidance or code of practice. You are also expected to make sure that team members follow procedures designed to protect them. This may include taking breaks when working with VDUs, wearing safety boots, lifting heavy items safely, using chemicals in an approved way and making a record of any accidents that happen. You may also want to be trained as a first aider so that you can deal confidently and effectively with any injuries that do happen.

Perhaps your most important task is to provide a model of best practice. You cannot expect your team to follow the rules if you do not. If you need help in identifying hazards at work or assessing the risk, or if you think that there are health and safety problems that need dealing with, speak to your manager, who may call on the advice of a health and safety officer or external consultant. Treat health and safety at work seriously – otherwise a life or limb could be lost.

## Summary

- A hazard is any activity, equipment or circumstance that could cause harm or injury. Risk is the chance that it might happen. Hazards cause accidents; risk is the likelihood that an accident will happen.

- The three most common causes of accidents at work are falling from heights, being hit or caught by a moving object or being hit by a falling object.

- The chances of being killed or injured at work are fairly low, but vary from industry to industry. Accidents at work usually happen because hazards exist and are not taken seriously or because some people behave in ways that increase risk.

- Risk assessments are used to identify the level (high, medium or low) and the type of risk, and to indicate the appropriate action.

- Organisations are advised to follow the hierarchy of control when attempting to reduce workplace risks.

- You have legal responsibilities for health and safety at work as an ordinary employee. As a team leader, you may have additional responsibility.

## Review your learning

- What are the main hazards and the risks associated with them in your workplace? (What could cause accidents and how likely are they to happen?)

- Are the risks high, medium or low?

- For the high and medium risks particularly, what steps have been taken to minimise the risk? Do you think these are adequate, could more be done, are safety rules and procedures followed properly?

- What action, if any, could you take to reduce the risks to health and safety at work?

- What personal development do you think you need at this point to improve your effectiveness as a protector of your team members' health and safety at work? If you feel that you have had sufficient training and refresher training at present, consider what you can do to keep yourself up to date with approved good practice.

You cannot expect your team to follow the rules if you do not.

# 19 | Using resources well

## Introduction

Teams are an organisation's way of grouping together people with the equipment and other things the team needs. In this chapter we look at two requirements that are common across all organisations, no matter what they do. The requirements are efficiency and effectiveness. We consider what they mean, why they are important and how they are measured. To start, however, we need to consider how teams use and combine resources to produce goods and services.

## Types of resource

All organisations need four basic types of resource to operate.

- People – sometimes called 'human resources', which some people consider to be an unpleasant description.

- Facilities – buildings, land and other facilities in which to operate.

- Equipment – machinery, tools, vehicles and other equipment to make goods or supply services.

- Consumables – power, energy or fuel, materials and other items needed to achieve the organisation's goals.

Some organisations also regard *information* about what they produce as a resource. As team leader, you are likely to be responsible for at least one, if not all, of these different types of resource. (Money is excluded from this list. It is needed, of course, to pay wages, rent buildings and so on, but its value is in the resources it buys.)

## The balance of resources

Organisations and their teams can combine resources in many ways and in varying proportions to produce the goods and services they supply. Some rely heavily on just one type of resource (intensive use). A steelworks is energy-intensive and a local council is usually labour-intensive, for example. Other organisations, such as hospitals and toolmaking companies, use resources in a more equal balance.

Why is this important? Because an organisation might be able to substitute one resource (like machines and equipment) for another resource (like labour) to reduce its costs. This has happened a lot in manufacturing, using automation to make parts and to assemble or paint them. In services it has also been happening, using information and communications technology (telephones and computers) to replace both people and buildings.

One of a team leader's responsibilities is to ensure that the team combines its resources to best effect, so that it produces the right quantity and quality of goods and services. This means being concerned about both the efficiency and the effectiveness of the team.

## Using resources efficiently

Efficiency is the relationship between the resources that are used ('input') and the quantity of goods and services ('output') that are produced. If fewer inputs are used to produce a particular output (product or service), then the output is produced more efficiently. This can be shown as a sum:

$$\text{Efficiency} = \frac{\text{Output}}{\text{Input}}$$

For example, if a team of eight people can produce 320 products an hour, then the efficiency of the team is:

$$\text{Efficiency} = \frac{320}{8} = 40 \text{ units per person}$$

Efficiency can be increased by:

* producing more output with the same inputs (people, equipment and so on)

* producing the same output with fewer inputs.

So, efficiency increases if, for example, people get better at what they do, use better equipment or cut waste, or if the land and buildings are better laid out or are more suitable for the work undertaken. By contrast, if resources are wasted or there is a lot of poor quality output that has to be thrown away or reworked, the efficiency is reduced. Training, changing the way the team works or changing the equipment and materials they work with are among ways of increasing efficiency.

You can measure the efficiency of only one resource at a time – the efficiency of people or a particular piece or type of equipment, for example. Measuring efficiency also depends on what you regard as your output. If it is getting as many nails into a piece of wood as possible, then the quantity of nails is the output and the number of 'nails per person' is the measure. But if the position of the nails and their ability to hold the piece of wood on the wall is important, that is a different measure. That is why you also need to be concerned about 'effectiveness'.

### What is the 'output'?

Many call centres measure the efficiency of customer service staff by counting the number of callers they deal with every hour. But David Mead, who was Customer Service Director at First Direct's call centre, said, "I just love our people talking to our customers as much as they want to talk." This was because he measured output by the satisfaction of customers, not by the number of them who were 'dealt with' during a shift.

# Using resources effectively

Effectiveness is concerned with what you are producing. Whereas efficiency is basically about quantity (of output per unit of input), effectiveness is about quality. There is more about quality in Chapter 21, but for the moment let us think of quality as being goods or services produced to the standard that we intended. Effectiveness is the measure of how well we are doing this.

Effectiveness can be measured in many ways, according to the industry. There are some examples in the box below. These measures of effectiveness are sometimes called performance indicators and they are concerned with how effective the organisation and the team are in producing what they intended to produce.

## Measuring effectiveness

| Activity | Measure of effectiveness |
| --- | --- |
| TV assembly line | Number of defective units produced on the assembly line |
| Fruit packing station | Proportion of apples graded class 1, class 2, class 3 |
| College of further education | Proportion of students who rate the teaching as 'good' or 'excellent' |
| Fire station | Proportion of emergency calls arrived at within 15 minutes of alarm |
| Insurance company call centre | Average waiting time for customers who telephone |
| Hospital surgical ward | Incidence of post-operative infection |

You can see that an assembly line that increases its production of televisions but also increases its reject rate may be more efficient but is also less effective. The college that has larger classes and more students who are less satisfied with their education and training is more efficient but less effective.

## When effectiveness can be sacrificed to efficiency

High levels of efficiency should not be at the expense of effectiveness, and there are occasions when it is right to sacrifice efficiency.

- In emergencies, it may be necessary to reduce efficiency to increase effectiveness. A hospital casualty department may keep people with minor injuries waiting longer for treatment if there is a coach crash and many people with serious injuries. The waiting time will go up (so that efficiency is decreased), but more lives will be saved (so that effectiveness is increased).

- Although it is not generally a good thing to do, where quality is well above the minimum required, it may be allowed to fall to cope with a surge in demand. As long as the standard is still within the limits people will tolerate (it is said to be 'within tolerance'), the reduced effectiveness of the team will not matter.

These are both exceptional cases and should only be temporary. Other than these cases, a team should always be trying to improve both its efficiency *and* its effectiveness.

## Summary

- Efficiency is the relationship between the resources that are used ('input') and the quantity of goods and services ('output') that are produced.

- Effectiveness is producing the output (of goods or services) to the standard of quality intended and is measured by performance indicators.

- Increases in efficiency should not be at the expense of effectiveness, except in rare circumstances.

## Review your learning

Look at the resources your team uses.

- Do you rely heavily on one particular type of resource? If so, which one?

- How does your organisation measure efficiency and effectiveness?

- Do you and your team look for ways to increase both of these?

- Do you ever sacrifice effectiveness (or efficiency) to ensure that a job gets done?

- Does your team ever sacrifice safety for efficiency? If so, what is your view of this?

- How would you go about changing the efficiency or effectiveness of your team? Who would you involve and how would you present any proposed changes to the team?

A team should always be trying to improve both its efficiency *and* its effectiveness.

# 20 | Keeping costs down

## Introduction

Every organisation needs money to meet its costs. As a team leader you need to recognise the main types of cost and what you can do to ensure that they are kept under control. In particular you need to distinguish between the costs that you can do something about and those that are largely outside your control. You also need to monitor your team's performance, making good use of the data collected.

## What are costs?

Cost, as you saw in Chapter 19, is the amount of money paid for using the resources such as:

- people (who get paid wages)
- tools, machinery and other equipment (that have to be bought, leased or rented, and also need maintenance and repair)
- buildings, land and facilities (that also need to be bought, leased or rented, and maintained)
- materials, power and other consumables (that have to be bought).

Some costs exist irrespective of how much an organisation produces. These are fixed costs (sometimes called overheads). Other costs arise because of what and how much is being produced. These are called variable (or direct) costs and they change as the type and level of production vary. Examples of both types of cost are shown in the box below.

---

### Fixed and variable costs

| Fixed costs (overheads) | Variable (direct) costs |
|---|---|
| • Buildings, land and facilities (eg. renting an office) | • Production staff and service staff (eg. assembly workers, delivery drivers or customer service staff) |
| • Machinery, tools and equipment (eg. buying a computer network) | • Materials, power and other consumables (eg. petrol, packaging, steel) |
| • Management, central administration, security | |

---

## Fixed costs

You cannot do very much about the level of fixed costs. They do not vary with output, so, even if your team produces nothing, fixed costs will still have to be paid. What you can do, however, is to ensure that the resources, like buildings and equipment that are part of the organisation's fixed costs, are used properly and as fully as possible (to get the most out of them). You should, for example, ensure that equipment is serviced and maintained well, to prolong its life. Most organisations put aside money every year to allow for the depreciation (wearing out) of buildings, machinery, vehicles and other equipment. Depreciation is generally based on the expected life of the items, which could be three years for a computer but 50 years for a building. By taking care of the resources you use, your team can give them extra life and help to reduce the organisation's fixed costs.

## Variable costs

Variable costs go up and down with the level of output. This is because power is being used to run equipment and to light and heat the workplace; materials are being used to produce goods or provide services; and the number and size of the teams actively providing goods and services vary in line with the level of production.

Team leaders have much more influence over the total variable costs by:

* reducing waste (improving quality so that fewer items are rejected, or conserving energy)

* helping team members to perform better (increasing their productivity) so that extra team members are not needed (which would push up variable costs).

Both of these will increase your team's efficiency and reduce variable costs, or increase output for the same costs.

## Reducing costs

You can help to keep variable costs down by encouraging team members to:

* develop their skills, to reduce faults and errors

* use their time better

* be careful in using materials or power (such as printing on both sides of paper when producing drafts of documents, or switching off engines when vehicles are stationary).

## Stock control

Reducing costs also includes stock (or inventory) control. It involves ensuring that items are stored correctly, safely and securely, especially in retailing where theft is a major cost. It also involves not allowing stock levels to exceed agreed limits or to drop below what is needed. Excess stock costs money because:

- it can deteriorate in storage so that it must be thrown away or sold off at a loss

- stock costs money to store, and storage areas can be very costly

- if the money used to buy stock has been borrowed, interest has to be paid on it.

However, letting stock levels get too low can disrupt production, waste time and disappoint customers. That is why a balance has to be struck, between too much and too little stock, based on a combination of:

- the minimum order that the supplier will accept

- the time it takes to supply

- the rate at which stock is used.

*Just in time*

Some organisations have reduced the ordering period between delivery and low stock levels by using a Just In Time (JIT) system. Parts are ordered to meet production requirements, with nothing held in reserve, and are delivered directly to the production line or cell just when they are needed.

## Understanding the supply chain

JIT relies on partnership arrangements between a customer and its suppliers. They work together to keep production flowing. These partnerships include the suppliers' suppliers, and even their suppliers, who together form the supply chain.

You should know where your organisation and your team's tasks lie in the supply chain. How flexible are your suppliers, how quickly can they supply the products or services your team needs? How many customers are there beyond your team, expecting flexibility and speedy responses from you? Understanding your position in the supply chain helps you to understand how dependent you are on suppliers, and the pressure you may get from your customers.

Even if you work in a service organisation, you may be able to improve the supply chain. Your customers may use their own equivalent of a JIT system – leaving it to the last minute – and expect goods and services to be available the moment they decide they want them. How rapid is the service that your team can provide? Your team needs to recognise how important it is to reduce any delays between the moment when customers place orders and the time when goods or services are delivered. The organisation must match what it supplies to its customers' demands if it is to meet their requirements (and, perhaps, stay in business). Public sector organisations, such as government departments, need to be just as responsive, because service users expect the same quality of service from them that they get elsewhere. Reducing delays, cutting stock levels and being responsive to customers all contribute to improving the team's productivity.

## Improving team productivity

Productivity is another word for efficiency and is generally used when talking about people. Your team's productivity is measured by how much each person produces, or how much the team as a whole produces. It can be improved by:

- increasing team members' skills (see Chapter 15)
- reorganising work patterns and methods (see Chapters 23 and 24)
- identifying barriers to efficient working.

*Identifying barriers to efficient working*
This could be the way that other people in the organisation work or the way that goods or services are supplied to you. You may not be able to change them, but you can tell your manager about the effect on your team's productivity.

## Dealing with poor performers

You may have productivity problems because of the poor performance of a team member. There can be many reasons for this. Team members might be completely out of their depth in the job, unaware that they are not doing what is expected, or suffering from ill health or from personal or family problems.

You should always be prepared to talk to someone who is not performing well and ask if they can identify any reasons. If appropriate, encourage the person to use any services that are available at work (for example in the HR or personnel department) or locally (perhaps they need to consult their doctor) to help them. They may need training or advice on their performance, which you may be able to organise or supply yourself.

If none of this helps, or if they will not acknowledge the problem or respond to what is offered, be prepared to discuss the problem with your manager.

## Monitoring performance

One of your responsibilities as team leader is to monitor your team's performance. This means knowing:

- if all your resources are being used well and fully
- how much is being produced
- whether what is produced meets quality standards.

You and your team are accountable for the way that you use buildings, equipment and consumables. As team leader, you may be responsible for ensuring that team members are present and working to the best of their abilities. This may mean recording and monitoring:

- team members' timekeeping and attendance
- the use and condition of equipment
- the use of consumables and stock levels.

You may also have to record the level of work output and, perhaps, analyse the data for patterns in the team's performance. However, tables of production, absenteeism or faulty goods figures are not easy to analyse or see patterns in. One way of seeing if the data is climbing or falling, or if there is some other pattern over time, is to convert the data to a graph such as the one on page 124.

Reduce any delays between the moment when customers place orders and the time when goods or services are delivered.

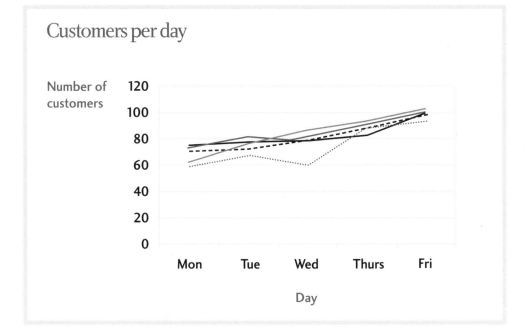

Customers per day

Number of customers

*(Graph showing number of customers, y-axis from 0 to 120 in increments of 20, x-axis showing Mon, Tue, Wed, Thurs, Fri labelled "Day")*

The graph shows the number of customers served by a team in a fast food restaurant during their afternoon and early evening shift. It is clear that sales increase from Monday to Friday, so the team could use the information to plan stock levels, schedule part-time team members and consider ways of promoting the restaurant on quiet days. (If you do not know how to produce or read charts or graphs you could ask to be trained to do so or ask for advice from someone in the organisation, such as a quality manager.)

## Goals, schedules and plans

Your team needs goals for your level of output and quality (customer satisfaction levels or reject rates, for example). You can also set goals for the resources you use. As you saw in Chapter 5, the best goals are SMART and stretching, and are agreed by the team (so that members are better motivated and much keener to raise performance because they feel more in control of their work).

### Planning to achieve your goals

You and the team need to plan *how* you are going to achieve your goals. A plan can be written down or it can be in your head, but it should say:

- what is going to be done
- which facilities, equipment and materials will be needed
- how it will be done
- who will do what
- when (and possibly where) it will be done.

Most importantly, your team members should have a chance to help you to decide on the plan and should all know what the plan is. Sometimes, if the task is fairly big and complex, then the plan may be quite general and the detailed tasks are then identified on a schedule (a miniature version of the plan, dealing with detail).

## Summary

- Costs occur because resources (people, buildings, equipment and consumables) are used. Some are fixed but others vary in line with output.

- Teams and team leaders can help to keep costs to a minimum by taking care of the equipment they use, reducing waste and increasing productivity.

- Waste can be reduced by improving skills, reducing equipment faults or human error, avoiding wasting time and using consumables with care. Stock should be kept to a practicable minimum (especially by systems like Just In Time) and stored safely and securely.

- Productivity can be increased by raising team members' skills, reorganising work patterns and methods, identifying barriers to efficient working and doing something about poor performers.

- Team leaders need to monitor the team's performance, to see which resources are being used, how much is produced and what the quality is. This is best done by agreeing SMART, stretch goals and targets against which actual performance is monitored, to identify areas for improvement.

## Review your learning

Look at the resources your team uses and identify those that generate fixed costs and those that generate variable costs.

- What can you do to reduce costs or to ensure that they are kept under better control?

- What could you and your team do to:

  - reduce waste

  - improve productivity?

- Think about how your team uses resources.

  - what targets are set for your team's use of resources, output and quality?

  - are these targets SMART?

  - do they stretch you and the team?

- How is performance monitored? Are you doing enough to monitor performance so that you can suggest ways of making improvements?

# 21 | Keeping the customers satisfied

## Introduction

Only a few staff deal directly with customers, but this does not mean that your team can forget about customers. A key role for team leaders is agreeing standards (or targets) with team members and managers so that you and your team are committed to achieving them. The closer the standards are to customer requirements, the more likely it is that customers will be satisfied with the goods and services they buy or use. This chapter looks at ways you can keep your team members customer-focussed, so that they are committed to meeting and, if possible, exceeding your customers' requirements.

## Who are your customers?

Customers may be external or internal, and may be known by other descriptions such as 'client', 'consumer', 'member' or 'stakeholder'.

### External

External customers are people outside the organisation who buy your organisation's goods and services. They may be individual members of the public (sometimes known as consumers) or they may be other organisations (sometimes called 'B2B' or 'business to business' customers). The other organisations may use the goods and services for themselves or use them to produce other goods and services. (You may know them as 'client organisations'). External customers also include pupils and their parents at a school; patients and their relatives in a hospital; the members of a professional institute; or the donors and beneficiaries of a charity. Even if you do not sell goods and services to them, thinking of them as 'customers' can help you to make their requirements a team priority.

### Internal

It is likely that you have customers inside the organisation too. These internal customers are the people and teams who rely on you and your team to do your team tasks effectively so that they can do theirs. In a factory, for example, a team might carry out one part of the process, before passing the work to other teams for them to complete. In a hospital you might provide cleaning or portering services to ward managers and their staff.

# What do your customers require?

It is the team leader's role to identify your internal and external customers. If you and your team do not deal directly with them, then talk to the people in your organisation who do. Find out what kind of customer buys your organisation's goods and services – old, young, male, female, single, with children, or a small, large local, national, regional or international business.

## How do you know what customers require?

Some organisations spend large amounts of money to find out what their customers require and how they judge quality. If your organisation does this, you may know or be able to find out what has been discovered about your customers. However, there are other ways of finding out, or at least getting a good idea about, what customers require. These include:

- observing customer behaviour
- analysing customer complaints and returns
- collecting feedback
- benchmarking – examining what high-performing (and customer-satisfying) organisations do, comparing this to your organisation's own procedures and making any appropriate changes
- analysing audit and inspection findings.

Ask yourself what your customers *require*. (This avoids debates about whether what they 'want' and what they 'need' are different.) Consider what they are looking for specifically – what it is about your product or service that they will judge it by. These are the quality characteristics. For example, a consumer buying a car may look at its carrying capacity and engine size, colour and trim choices, its 'looks', the car's and the car maker's image (although they may be reluctant to admit to this), the costs of servicing and parts, and the way that sales staff behave.

*Price and quality*
Customers are, of course, concerned about price, but their buying decisions are based on how well the products or services match their requirements at a particular price. People usually pay more for something that most closely matches their requirements. Only where all the products and services offered are identical in meeting these requirements will price become the deciding factor.

Price and quality are related, of course. Customers create hierarchies of requirements – an order of priority – with the most important quality characteristics at the top of the hierarchy. This is why a customer who normally buys from a supplier with a slow but cheap delivery may switch to buying from another more expensive supplier selling almost identical items when a fast delivery is needed. Speed has jumped from low to high in the hierarchy of requirements, displacing cost.

The ideal situation to be in is to be able to meet a customer's requirements fully, to offer all the preferred quality characteristics and to be able to compete on price. This is where standards and teams come in.

> Ask yourself what your customers *require.*

## Requirements and standards

It is important to recognise the difference between 'requirements' and 'standards':

- customers judge your performance by their requirements – the quality characteristics they seek

- organisations set standards (or targets) to judge their own performance.

Most organisations have a large number of customers, all of whom have slightly different requirements and so look for different quality characteristics. This is one reason for being flexible, to be able to offer some variety to meet these different requirements. However, you cannot hope to meet every requirement in fine detail, and this makes judging your performance difficult. Even so, you can set standards that reflect these requirements and aim to be consistent in producing goods or supplying services that meet these standards. There are some examples of requirements and standards in the box below.

---

### Customer requirements and standards

| The customer requires: | The organisation's standards: |
|---|---|
| **Prompt, efficient and effective service** | • **Telephone answered within two minutes of call** |
| | • **Customer welcomed and given agent's name** |
| | • **Agent takes responsibility for exploring any problems and ensuring they are dealt with within 24 hours** |
| **Attractive-looking products that work when installed and last for at least five years** | • **100% testing at end of production line** |
| | • **0.001 % (one in one hundred thousand) with operating defects** |
| | • **No external visible scratches or faults** |

---

### Targets

Targets are really just another word for standards but they tend to be standards that are expressed as numbers. They are often less than one hundred per cent – for example, '80% of patients are seen within 3 hours' or '95% of customers say they are satisfied or very satisfied with the service they received'.

### External standards

External standards are also a way of measuring how well your organisation meets the general requirements of your customer. Some of these are assessed by external inspectors or auditors, others are assessed by the organisation itself. Some examples are shown in the box opposite.

## External quality standards

| | |
|---|---|
| ISO* 9000 | This international standard defines quality assurance procedures so that customers can be confident that they are in place. |
| ISO* 14000 | This is an international environmental standard to assess the impact an organisation has on the environment and the precautions it takes to minimise this impact. |
| Investors in People (IiP) | This UK standard defines best practice in identifying and meeting employees' development needs that enable the organisation to meets its goals. |
| EFQM Business Excellence | This self-assessment standard enables organisations to identify how well their management and systems enable them to meet the standards of the best managed European organisations. |

* ISO is the International Standards Organisation, based in Switzerland. Its members are national standards bodies, such as the British Standards Institute (BSI).

# Setting customer-focussed standards

It can be hard to set standards for some customer requirements – and they tend to be important requirements. Being 'treated with care and consideration' by doctors and nurses in a hospital might be what most patients want, but how do you set appropriate standards? In part it can be done by talking to people in particular ways, explaining what you need to do and asking permission before doing it. But it can probably be measured only by asking a sample of patients whether they feel they were treated with care and consideration. Aiming for 95% who say 'Yes' is the standard or target.

As you saw in Chapter 5, standards or targets have to be measurable to be worth setting. If you cannot measure your performance, you cannot judge it. The standards or targets should also be achievable. It is claimed that some school and hospital targets are impossible to achieve so that some schools enter only those pupils for exams who they think are bound to pass, and some hospitals have a concerted effort to reduce casualty waiting times in the week that they are to be measured.

## Relying on the team

One way to ensure that customer targets and standards are achievable is to involve the people who are responsible for achieving them in setting them. Team leaders should agree standards/targets and goals with team members and managers so that everyone has an investment in making them work. The closer standards or targets are to customer requirements, the more likely it is that customers will be satisfied with the goods and services they buy or use – provided that those standards are achieved. To match your team's performance standards as closely as possible to customer requirements, you and the team should:

> Look for ways to improve what you do, so that you continuously raise standards.

- find out what (internal or external) customers require – this may involve collaboration with other people or teams

- set standards or targets that reflect those requirements and that you believe you can achieve

- work to achieve those standards and targets consistently

- look for ways to improve what you do, so that you continuously raise standards.

As a team leader, this is where you can make one of your most important contributions and help your team to become a high-performing one. The next chapter looks at how you can create a team that is responsive to customer needs and able to produce the goods and services they require.

## Summary

- Your team should satisfy the requirements of its external customers and internal customers as far as is possible.

- Customers judge your organisation's goods and services against sets of quality characteristics that reflect their requirements. The requirements have different priorities and may vary from time to time.

- You, your team and your organisation can identify customer requirements and set measurable, achievable standards to satisfy them.

- Your team needs goals and standards/targets to define what you are aiming to achieve in order to meet customers' requirements. They are what you, your team and your organisation measure your performance against.

- Being customer-focussed involves identifying what customers require, setting and consistently achieving standards that reflect those requirements, and looking for ways to improve performance and raise standards.

## Review your learning

- Who are your internal and external customers?

- How do you know what they require? Who do you need to speak with in the organisation, and what methods for finding out customer requirements might be most appropriate for your sector, organisation and team?

- What standards or targets do you work to? How well do these reflect customers' requirements and priorities?

- How well do you achieve these standards or targets?

- How can you involve team members more in setting and achieving customer requirements?

# 22 | Creating a flexible team

## Introduction

Teams can bring flexibility to the way goods and services are produced, so that they meet customers' requirements more closely. This chapter considers the advantages to an organisation of having teams that can work flexibly and shows how flexible working is often part of a technique called 'cell' (or 'zone') working.

## Flexible production

People have become far choosier about what they buy. They want goods and services that meet their specific requirements. Until mass production arrived, most goods and services used to be produced for individual customers in a craft or jobbing production system. Mass production changed all this as very large factories produced identical products in huge volumes at much lower cost than a craft system could achieve. Now craft or jobbing production tends to be used only with high-value items where customers can afford to pay for something exclusive, such as designer clothes, or where the market is small, as with building power stations, for instance. Mass production is now the norm.

Many people want products and services that suit them personally, as if they were produced just for them, but at mass production prices. This has led to the process of 'mass customisation', where standard products are produced with large numbers of variations that can be included as the product or service is produced. Cars coming down the same production line can all be fitted with different equipment and be different colours, each one slightly different from the one in front and the one behind. A travel firm can put together holiday packages comprising different flights, different locations, car hire and other extras, all based on standard services.

### Mass customisation at Dell

Dell revolutionised the market for personal computers (PCs) by not holding any stock of finished products. Each computer is made to order, using standard components. The customers decide which of the different parts they want in their machine and these are then combined and the PC is despatched. Dell also holds as few stocks of components as the company dares. Each time a customer decides on a particular component, this is allocated from stock and, when the number falls to a particular level, replacements are ordered. This also helps to keep costs down.

Customisation is all about flexibility, being able to adapt what is available from a menu of choices. The greater the choice available, the greater the level of customisation. Flexibility is easier if people can co-operate, help one another, focus on the goal (satisfying customers' requirements) and make decisions without asking their managers. These are all the things that teams are good at.

## Cell or zone working

Flexible teams providing customised goods and services are a feature of some of the most successful organisations, but in every case the flexibility is built upon other approaches, such as continuous improvement (see Chapter 23) and Just In Time. One particular approach that relies on teams and is also often associated with flexible working is cell or zone working.

Originally often used in manufacturing (and increasingly by service providers), cell or zone working is designed to help to meet customer requirements more closely. Conventional ways of organising resources put all the same activities together, so that goods and services for different customers follow each other through the same plastics moulding, painting or assembly line, or through the same insurance claim handling, investigation and finance operations. Cell working combines these operations so that the whole production operation to produce goods or services for a particular customer (or group of customers) is integrated.

## Two examples of cell production

1. In a packaging company a single cell moulds plastic tubes for denture cleaning tablets, prints the tubes and packs them. Previously the plastic was moulded on a plastics production line, moved to the printing department and waited behind other printing work. Now a single cell has responsibility for the whole process and for meeting the customer's quality requirements.

2. An insurance company used to sort all claims in one office, log them on the computer system and enter the full details of each claim, pass them to investigations (where a claim for a damaged carpet waited behind one for a multi-million pound factory fire) and, if accepted, sent them to finance for payment. Now claims are initially logged, sorted and sent to individual cells that specialise in different types of claim. The cell team collects the details of the claim, investigates it and, if accepted, pays the customer.

## Taking responsibility

Cell working often relies on team members being able and willing to perform different tasks and learn new skills so that they can meet customers' requirements as quickly and as well as possible. When goods or services are produced in separate specialist departments they can spend days or weeks waiting between stages while other goods and services are processed. By giving teams of people with different skills the responsibility for the whole process, these delays can be reduced. The team also has full responsibility for quality and for delivering on time rather than sharing it between different departments, all expecting the other to take responsibility. To work well, cell working needs flexible teams, not tied to a single way of working but willing to try different ways and, most importantly, committed to meeting customers' needs.

*Encouraging flexibility*

The experience of cell working gives clues to any team leader. If you can help your team to be more flexible, it is likely to perform better. Your main role in this is likely to be by:

- recognising the importance of meeting customers' requirements

- encouraging people to develop their skills and by helping them to learn

- looking constantly for opportunities to improve how you work as a team.

Above all, it is about accepting responsibility for all this, a responsibility that the team needs to share with the team leader. When team leaders can say 'We will do this', their managers and customers know that they can rely on them to do it. Real teams, willing and able to work flexibly, can make this possible.

> Flexibility is easier if people can co-operate, help one another, focus on the goal (satisfying customers' requirements) and make decisions without asking their managers.

## Summary

- People want individualised products and services at mass production prices.

- Team working can help to achieve the flexibility required to meet customer requirements.

- Cell or zone working is increasingly used to ensure that responsibility for quality, delivery and other customer requirements is shared by the team of people working together to produce the goods or provide the service.

## Review your learning

- How is your team's work organised? Are you involved in mass production or in one-off or limited-run production?

- Do you work in a specialist department or division responsible for part of the production of goods or a service, or are you part of a cell team, responsible for the whole process?

- How far are you able to customise what you offer to meet individual needs?

- How much flexibility are you and your team allowed in how you undertake the tasks you perform?

- Would greater team flexibility improve your team's performance? If so, how can you go about encouraging flexibility?

# 23 | Is there a problem?

## Introduction

It is crucial for teams to have clear standards for their work that reflect what internal or external customers require. Despite your best efforts, however, there may be times when you and your team encounter problems in achieving those standards. This chapter looks at ways to monitor your performance, find out what is causing a problem and what you and your team can do about it.

## When things go wrong

Problems that could stop the team from meeting customer requirements include:

- late delivery of essential materials, parts or services

- a breakdown or wrong setting on equipment

- sickness or absenteeism among team members

- poor performance among some team members, due to insufficient skills, a lack of commitment or motivation, or personal problems

- an emergency or crisis that could not be forecast, such as power failure, fire or flood.

When these or other problems occur, you need to distinguish between those that you and your team can do something about and those that are outside your control.

## What can the team do something about?

**Problems you can do something about yourselves**

- **Poor operation of equipment**

- **Lack of skill**

- **Poor relationships in the team**

- **Tasks wrongly allocated**

- **Team members not knowing what is expected of them**

**Problems you need other people to do something about**

- **Suppliers badly selected**

- **Badly designed production systems in the organisation**

- **Poorly made products and low standard services bought for your team to use**

- **Emergencies or crises, like power failures or snowdrifts**

You should concentrate the team's energies on the problems they can do something about. Some problems may need you to bring together all the people involved, perhaps as a quality circle (see page 21). If the problem lies with an external supplier, then the team responsible there could be invited to discuss the problem with your team.

## Monitoring performance

Some problems are immediately obvious – like a breakdown of machinery. Others can be prevented if there are systems of feedback in place to alert you in good time. Feedback is information flowing back to you about your actions (see page 69). The feedback could be informal, such as a customer complaint by phone, or a formal system for collecting data on performance as part of the quality control of products and services.

Quality control is the system to ensure that products and services are to the desired standard. It consists of four steps.

1. Set standards (and targets) for performance.

2. Monitor performance to check what is being produced or supplied.

3. Compare what is produced against the standards.

4. Take action if performance fails to meet the standards.

### Set standards
Standards and targets (see Chapter 21) describe the quality of the product or service that the team should produce or supply consistently to meet customer requirements.

### Monitor performance
Monitoring (see pages 123-124) may include observation, automatic data collection or the keeping of records of what the team has done and how effective it was.

### Compare output with standards
By collecting data and analysing them, the team can identify when things are going wrong. The basis for any analysis should be what you intended to do – your standards.

### Take action
The whole point of quality control is to do something. Without action the previous three stages are a waste of time and effort.

> You should concentrate the team's energies on the problems they can do something about.

## Effective monitoring systems

A good monitoring system needs to balance all three of the following:

- low cost (because resources should be spent on *doing* not measuring)

- validity (so that it can measure what it is important to measure)

- promptness (so that you get feedback as soon as possible and can take action fast).

If it takes several weeks to get feedback on today's performance, or what you measure is what is *easy* to measure rather than what is *important*, or measurement costs nearly as much as producing the goods or services, then you have to ask whether the monitoring is worth it. Consider what you measure and ask yourself, is this what is really important for our customers? Does it lead to improvement as soon as it is practicable to do so? If monitoring does not help the team to meet customer requirements, you may need to discuss with your team and your manager how monitoring can be improved.

## A control chart

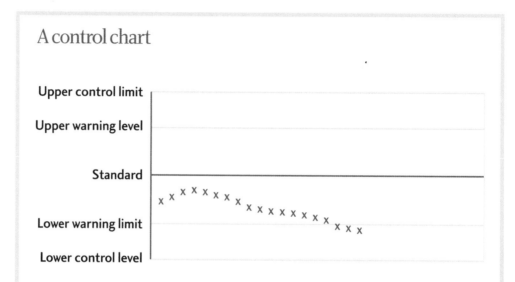

Manufacturing organisations often have clear quality control systems. They might check every product as it is produced, or they may check a sample of products in each batch. The use of control charts helps them to monitor a particular standard and to warn them of problems. There is usually an acceptable level of variation (called the 'tolerance'), within which there is no problem. This control chart shows quality that is a little below standard, but is still within the tolerance allowed. However, the gradual deterioration suggests that quality is slipping out of control and that something needs to be done.

Of course, not all aspects of quality can be measured so easily. Some, like how well team members serve customers, can best be judged by observing performance. Numbers are useful for measuring many aspects of performance, but as a team leader your judgement about quality (a form of monitoring), based on your knowledge and experience, may be just as important.

## Why are things going wrong?

The only way you can do something about quality is to find out *why* problems are occurring. Problem solving is most effective when it is both:

- based on facts (ideally recorded ones), not opinions
- is team-based (to take advantage of members' knowledge and experience).

It is a good idea to collect data, present the data visually, analyse the problem with the team, and identify and implement solutions with the team. The rest of this chapter considers ways to do this, while Chapter 24 looks at ways to identify and implement solutions.

## Collect data

You cannot solve a quality problem if you do not know what the problem is, its size or how often it occurs, so you need information about all those aspects of team performance that matter to your customers. If there are no data being collected formally, then you can do it yourself. The simplest way is by keeping a simple, manual record of each time the problem occurs, using a 'gate count' (see box below). Record each event (such as a defect or a customer complaint) by drawing a short vertical stroke. When you reach the fifth event, make the fifth stroke a diagonal from bottom right to top left, so that it looks like a gate. This makes it easy to add and keep count.

| Gate counting | day | Count | Total |
|---|---|---|---|
| | 1 | ‖‖‖ ‖‖‖ ‖‖‖ ‖‖ | 17 |
| | 2 | ‖‖‖ ‖‖‖ ‖ | 11 |
| | 3 | ‖‖‖ ‖‖‖‖ | 9 |
| | 4 | ‖‖‖ ‖‖‖ ‖‖‖ | 13 |
| | 5 | ‖‖‖ ‖‖‖ ‖‖‖ ‖‖‖ ‖ | 21 |
| | 6 | ‖‖‖ ‖‖‖ ‖‖‖ | 15 |
| | 7 | | |
| | 8 | | |
| | 9 | | |
| | 10 | | |

## Present the data visually

It's often tricky to make sense of tables of numbers. The best way to show people the size of the problem, how often it occurs and if there are any patterns in the data is usually to create a graph or bar chart. These are quite easy to produce by hand or by using computer spreadsheets, (or you can ask your quality manager to do it for you). The important thing is to be able to see patterns in the information.

Three examples on page 138 show how data can be displayed. The first (the scatter graph) shows how delivery time increases in line with order size, so that the biggest orders take longest to deliver. The second (a bar chart) shows the different reasons for defects in products, in order of importance.

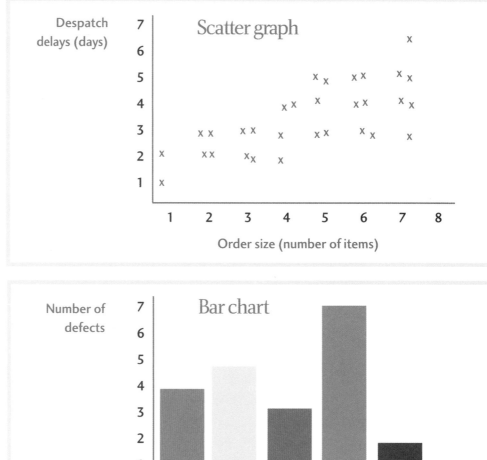

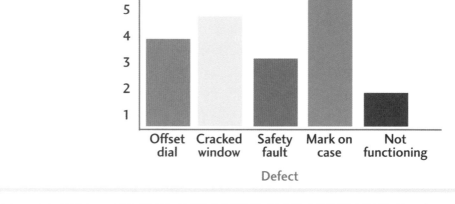

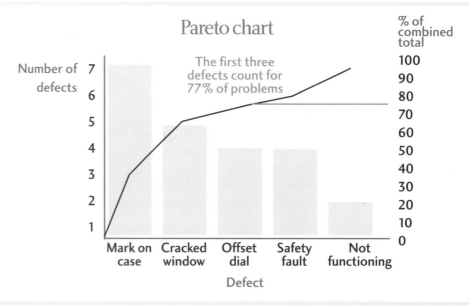

The third (a Pareto chart) is the most complex. There is a bar chart, showing the number of defects of each type, from the most common to the least common. Over this is a line graph, which shows what proportion of the combined types of defect are accounted for by the listed types of defect. The first defect ('mark on case'), for example, accounts for nearly 40% of the total defects (read this from the right-hand axis). The first and the second types of fault ('cracked window' and 'offset dial') together account for 60% of the total. The graph shows clearly that the three most common defects combined account for 77% – just over three-quarters of the total. These three can be considered as the 'significant few'; the others the 'trivial many'. This pattern is common in many organisations. Just a few defects cause the most problems. Dealing with them will solve more than three-quarters of the problems.

## Analyse the problem

Collecting data helps you to know the size and frequency of a problem, while presenting the data visually helps to reveal the patterns to everyone. Even so, the graphs cannot say *why* something is happening. There are two techniques that may help you to detect the cause of a problem – process flow charts and cause and effect diagrams.

## Process flow charts

The easiest way to examine what you do is to prepare a process flow chart. This helps everyone to have a clear idea about exactly what you are supposed to do (which may not always be the case) and helps to pinpoint where problems occur – delays, for example. You may need the help of your line manager or quality manager to draw the first process flow chart, then you will find subsequent ones quite easy to complete. There are a lot of different symbols you can use but the most commonly used are shown in the chart on the right.

## Cause and effect diagram

Cause and effect diagrams are sometimes called 'fishbone diagrams' (because of how they look ) or

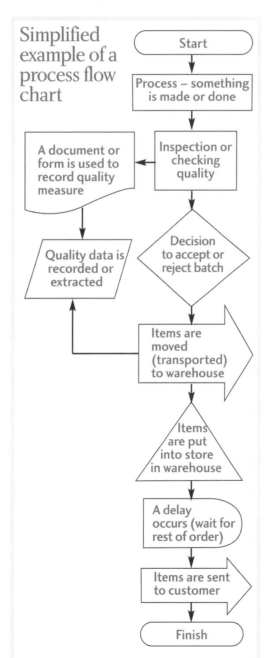

Simplified example of a process flow chart

'Ishikawa diagrams' (after the Japanese inventor). They help you to look at what *causes* the problems, so that you do not waste time trying to cure the symptoms (or consequences) instead. You start by labelling the problem in a box (see below) and show the 'spine' pointing at it, with four main 'bones' that you label with categories such as:

- people (for problems related, for example, to skills, absenteeism, motivation, poor team relationships and not knowing the quality standards)

- tools/equipment (breakdowns, faults, poor maintenance, wrong tools, insufficient or old tools)

- inspection/monitoring (for example, wrong aspects being monitored, data arriving too late, poorly presented, too many errors)

- materials/systems (faulty parts and consumable items, poorly designed procedures and lack of communication, for example).

These four main categories can be changed, but most problems tend to fall under these headings.

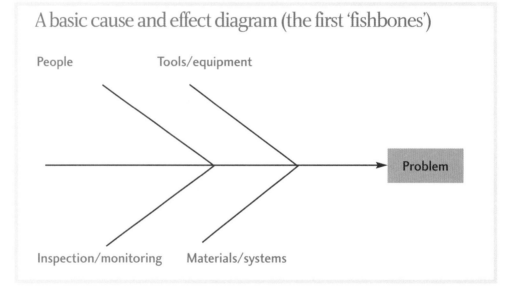

A basic cause and effect diagram (the first 'fishbones')

People          Tools/equipment

Problem

Inspection/monitoring     Materials/systems

Once the first fishbones are drawn, the team members then brainstorm (see Chapter 24) on the cause of the problem. Their list of ideas is then organised into the four categories and added to the diagram as small 'bones' coming off the four main ones (see opposite). Where one cause leads to another, it can be shown as a smaller 'bone'. For example, 'poor workmanship' is caused by 'inadequate training' and 'faulty tools' is caused by 'poor maintenance'. (It is often best to start by using small, removable, self-adhesive stickers.) Again, your line manager or quality manager should be able to help you at first, but you will soon find that it is not at all difficult to do.

Of course, all this has done is to tell you what the real problem is, the root cause of the failure to meet quality standards. What you now have to do is to rectify the problem, and this is what Chapter 24 is about.

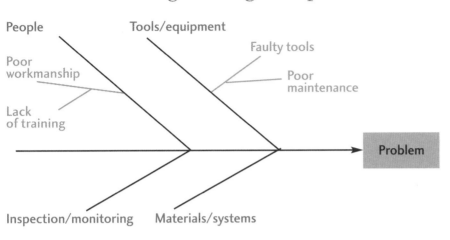

A cause and effect diagram being developed

**People** — Poor workmanship, Lack of training

**Tools/equipment** — Faulty tools, Poor maintenance

**Inspection/monitoring**

**Materials/systems**

**Problem**

## Summary

- Improving quality starts by understanding whether you and your team can do something about it or whether it is a problem that needs to involve people outside the team.

- You need to collect feedback on your performance to recognise how well you are meeting customers' requirements.

- Monitoring performance is part of the quality control process, involving setting standards, monitoring performance, comparing with standards and taking action.

- Monitoring systems should be valid, low in cost and give prompt feedback.

- Data are often easier to understand by using scatter graphs, bar charts or Pareto charts.

- You can analyse how your team works by using process flow charts. You can analyse the root cause of problems by producing cause and effect (fishbone) diagrams.

## Review your learning

- Does your organisation monitor performance against standards? If so, is the system of monitoring valid, low cost and prompt?

- Do you use data to help you to understand the nature, size and frequency of the problems? Is this information presented in ways that enable you to identify patterns in performance and problems? If not, what could you do to collect and present data to help your team to recognise problems more easily?

- Do you use structured ways of analysing the problems? If not, which techniques could you use?

# 24 | Improving performance

## Introduction

You and your team need to find solutions to problems at work, so that you close the gap between what the team does and what your customers require. This chapter suggests some simple techniques to encourage creativity and innovation in solving problems and considers what you can do to exceed customers' expectations. Most importantly, you will learn just how important teams and leadership really are.

## From problem to improvement

Chapter 23 outlined a few of the techniques for finding the cause of problems. But finding out why things are going wrong is only part of the process of continuous improvement. (This is sometimes called kaizen, meaning 'change for the better'.) Originally developed in Japan, 'continuous improvement' means that you are always looking for ways to do things well. Once standards have been met, they should be raised to do things even better. Continuous improvement means looking for ways to change small aspects of performance all the time, rather than necessarily trying to make one dramatic change.

'Continuous improvement' is itself part of a wider approach to quality called 'Total Quality Management' (TQM). The approach emphasises the importance of:

- defining quality in terms of customer requirements

- setting standards and monitoring performance

- using teams to solve problems and finding ways to improve performance continuously.

## Creative problem solving

Sometimes the solution to a problem is obvious. At other times the cause lies outside your direct control – another team is slow in their part of the process, for instance – so you need to resolve the problems with the other team, probably with the involvement of your manager. However, some problems need a more innovative approach because the solution is not obvious. This is where you can unleash the creative abilities of your team.

Everyone is capable of being creative, but many people are afraid to be so for fear of being laughed at or ignored. You need to encourage your team's creativity by making clear that you want them to be as original as they can be. There are several ways you can encourage this:

- brainstorming
- association
- benchmarking.

*Brainstorming*

This involves getting everyone in the team together and encouraging them to tell the group their ideas. There are two stages. In the first stage you encourage as many ideas as possible. At this point you are aiming for quantity, not quality, of ideas. The ideas can be practical, unrealistic, uneconomic, fantastical – it doesn't matter at first, because you are trying to trigger other ideas. You (or another member of the team) write the ideas on a whiteboard or flipchart, without comment. It is crucial in this first stage that there are no challenges: no matter how much people may disagree with an idea, they must not say anything about it yet. Keep the team going, by encouraging suggestions, until everyone is exhausted. (Some of the best ideas may come at the end.) The second stage is to sort and evaluate the ideas (see page 144): this is when you need to encourage discussion and a practical view of things.

*Association*

This is often better if you have some team members who are not confident enough to put forward their ideas as part of a brainstorming session. Instead, get them to sit in a circle and ask each one to write three ideas at the top of a sheet of paper. They then pass the sheet on around the circle three places, and write three more ideas on the new sheet under the existing three. The existing ideas on each sheet spark off new ideas. Repeat this until people have run out of ideas.

*Benchmarking*

As you saw on page 127, this involves comparing your team's performance with the way in which other successful teams and organisations perform, and using their experience as a basis for your own solutions. Sometimes the best ideas come from looking at organisations that are dissimilar. A car service and repair centre could look at a hospital casualty ward, for example, to see how they deal with everything from major injuries (a car involved in a crash) to someone needing an X-ray (a minor service).

## Creative problem solving at work

A factory had a problem with a machine. It was very sensitive to light and kept producing faulty products because there was so much natural sunlight in the factory. The manufacturers of the equipment could only recommend blocking all the natural light (from glass panels in the ceiling) and installing artificial lights, a solution that many other companies had used. The cost would be nearly £30,000. The cell team worked on the problem, asking themselves where else natural sunlight had to be blocked out. One member, a keen gardener, said that he hung a material known as 'shade netting' in his greenhouse to stop strong summer sunlight burning his prize plants. A sheet was bought for £20 and strung under the skylight in that part of the factory. The result? No more quality problems and a saving for the company of £29,980.

### Sorting ideas

The techniques of brainstorming, association and benchmarking can generate lots of original ideas. The challenge is to narrow them down to a workable solution. You can help to do this by agreeing *how* you are going to choose a solution before generating all the ideas. These are your 'selection criteria'. Your criteria might, for example, state that the solution must have four characteristics:

- have no cost
- use existing equipment
- be quick to introduce
- at least halve the reject rate.

If you do *not* decide the selection criteria at the outset, you could get bogged down in discussion about what they should be during the sorting process.

Check the team members' ideas against the selection criteria to find those that meet all of them (or those that meet the most). Then evaluate each in turn. This involves working through the ideas that have survived the selection process to compare the advantages and disadvantages of each. You can do this by discussion and consensus, or by voting.

In all this, from generating ideas through to sorting the ideas, you need to *lead* the team. Do not try to solve the problem yourself but use the collective abilities of the team and just guide them through the process.

> Involving people in identifying why and how to change, and in planning the change, will make them feel less threatened.

## Planning action

Once you have come up with the preferred solution, the team needs to work out how to put it into action, although you may need to discuss it with your manager before you can go ahead. Create an action plan that lists the tasks that need to be undertaken. The action plan should make it clear:

- what needs doing
- how it will be done
- who will do it
- when (and possibly where) it will be done.

Your task, as team leader, is to make sure that the agreed tasks are carried out properly and on time. Then, once the solution is in place, you need to monitor the team's performance and make any changes to ensure it provides the solution to your quality problem. The American quality guru W Edwards Deming called this the 'PDCA' (Plan, Do, Check, Action) cycle:

- plan what you are going to do
- do it
- check it is working
- take any necessary action to refine it.

Why the PDCA *cycle*? Because once you have improved the process, you should start it all over again. This is what continuous improvement means.

## Recognising barriers to change

It is not always easy to change how you and your team do things. But that is no reason not to try. You should also talk to your manager and to those people who can make changes to see how they could help you and your team to improve.

### Fear of change is a barrier

People tend to resist change simply because it means doing things differently, and they fear the unknown. They are worried that they may not be able to perform in a new role or learn new skills. You will recall from Chapter 14 that self-esteem is an important part of people's mental make-up. Change can unsettle them because it may affect how they are seen by others and how they see themselves.

### People in the team can be a barrier

People are often less frightened of something completely new if they can admit their lack of knowledge and skill, than of something only slightly different where they feel they ought to be competent. It is your responsibility as team leader to create a supportive team culture.

### People outside the team can be a barrier

Some barriers to change may be put up by people outside the team who are unsupportive or who may even deliberately set out to obstruct you. This can reflect their own fear of change and the threat to their self-esteem. It can also be due to their fear of losing power if you are able to make changes that they cannot control. Do not ignore such barriers. Be prepared to assert your team's right to make change, without being aggressive.

### Resources can be a barrier

Some barriers may be practical ones. The equipment you use may not be appropriate, the work layout may be wrong or the training you need may not be available. You need to be clear about what is wrong and what changes are needed, before you can work towards overcoming such barriers.

## Overcoming barriers to change

You can overcome some of these barriers by using creative problem-solving processes. Involving people in identifying why and how to change, and in planning the change, will make them feel less threatened. Admitting your own fears and weaknesses can also help people to realise that they are not alone, and by working collectively you can help to support one another.

If doing something about these barriers will cost money, you and the team need to put together a case supporting any expenditure that is needed. Try not to ask for new resources without knowing what the cost will be. Your case should show how any cost will be paid back through reduced costs or higher quality. Showing that you can justify money being spent will bolster your team's case and your reputation as a team leader with your managers and your team.

# Improvement is about more than just quality

In Chapter 19 you learnt the difference between *efficiency* (reducing waste and getting the most out of the resources your team uses – their productivity) and *effectiveness* (producing goods and services to the right standard, or quality). So far, continuous improvement has been described as being about quality (effectiveness) but it can be just as much about efficiency. You should be looking for ways to reduce waste and improve productivity alongside ways to improve quality. The two should go hand in hand.

As markets get more and more competitive and as the demand for public services increases, all organisations need to look for ways to cut their costs without reducing their quality. Your team can play an active part in making sure that you are constantly looking for ways to produce more and better goods and services with the resources available to you. This is also what continuous improvement means.

## Using your team

Throughout *Leading Teams* we have considered teams to be groups of people with different skills working together in an organised way to achieve their shared goals. We have seen that team members have two sets of role – task-related roles that involve using their skills to undertake the tasks that the team is there to perform, and team-related roles that help the team to function effectively. Every team member should also accept the team role involved in helping to improve quality and reduce costs (improve effectiveness and efficiency). What is more, it will help people to work together as a team and feel committed to the organisation if they can play an active part in improving what they do and how they do it.

## Develop your team leadership skills

You can also use continuous improvement as a way of developing yourself as a team leader, by practising different skills and inviting feedback from the team on your performance. Remember John Kotter's idea about leadership in Chapter 6 (on pages 36 and 37)? He says that leaders:

- establish direction

- align people

- motivate and inspire.

You can establish direction by having a vision of continuous improvement and by using some of the ideas in *Leading Teams* to achieve it. You can align people by getting the whole team alongside you in working to achieve the vision, and you can motivate and inspire team members by actively involving the team in making changes happen.

You can do this by, for example, using creative problem solving and action-centred leadership (the three-circle model featured in Chapter 7) techniques – focussing in on the task (the need to improve), the team (actively involved in improvement) and the individual (by recognising that everyone has something to contribute and can learn from one another). In the process you develop your leadership style and encourage participation, drawing on all the skills needed in the team leader role, listed on page 47. The most important of the skills you will use are your communication and personal presentation skills. If you feel anxious about playing a leading role with your team, tell them, and ask them to help and support you.

## Develop your team

One of the key outcomes of continuous improvement is the development of a multi-skilled team. By raising skill levels you increase flexibility (which can improve productivity and quality) and the ability to respond to the market. This can involve you in identifying the skills people need, training and coaching team members (or supporting other members to do it) and developing their own skills as well.

You will also be building the team by involving team members in agreeing goals to improve efficiency (because having shared goals is an important part of team working). A goal of reducing waste or increasing productivity can be set alongside reducing reject rates and increasing customer satisfaction. By having demanding but achievable (stretch) goals your team members will have the incentive to work more effectively together.

Of course, change can be challenging and some people may find it difficult to accept that they should play an active part in identifying changes in their own work role, or have different ideas about what improvement is needed. You need to be prepared to be assertive and deal with conflict, and to use your leadership skills to encourage acceptance of any changes that are needed.

## 'Delight' your customers

It is crucial to understand what your customers require and set performance standards that reflect those requirements. If everybody in the organisation is working towards those goals, then the organisation is more likely to be successful in competitive world markets. However, as more and more organisations are trying to do the same, those that stand out from the crowd have the best chance of success. This is why many organisations are not just trying to *satisfy* their customers' requirements but to *delight* them. 'Delight' usually involves providing customers with a better level of service than they dare to expect. It does not matter if you are in the public, private, mutual or charitable sector, you can always be looking for ways to add something to the service you provide that makes your customers recognise that you really do care about them.

It does not necessarily mean spending extra money. It is mainly about being willing to *listen* to your customers and understand their point of view, so that you can make their lives easier, make your product or service meet their needs more closely, or add that little something that they did not expect. If your team sets itself the highest standards of performance, then members will be motivated to delight their customers because that will confirm their team success. But to do this they need to be shown the way, to be given the direction and to be helped to achieve the highest goals. That is your role. That is leading teams.

> Many organisations are not just trying to *satisfy* their customers' requirements but to *delight* them.

# Summary

- Every team is capable of creativity in solving problems. You can encourage creativity by using techniques like:

    - brainstorming to generate lots of ideas without discussion

    - association, a similar technique that is less threatening for some people

    - benchmarking, using ideas and examples from other organisations and teams.

- Teams need to sort their ideas by agreeing clear criteria in advance.

- Plan how you will put the team's ideas into action and check that they are working. Remember PDCA (Plan, Do, Check, Action).

- Overcome barriers to change inside the team by involving people, recognising their fear and supporting them. Be assertive with people outside the team who erect unnecessary barriers, and prepare a clear business case for any expenditure needed.

- Continuous improvement is about effectiveness (improving quality) and also about efficiency (reducing waste and improving productivity).

- Continuous improvement helps you and the members of your team to develop your skills and to build a high-performing team.

# Review your learning

What are you going to do to improve your own performance as a team leader and to improve your team's performance? Think about your personal goals and your team's goals and discuss with your manager how you can develop a commitment to quality and customer focus by developing a culture of continuous improvement.

# Further help

If you want to explore further the topics covered in this book, you might like to follow up some of these suggestions.

- The Institute of Leadership & Management (ILM) has a wide and growing range of learning resources. Details are available from the ILM's website at www.i-l-m.com

- The website of the Center for Collaborative Organizations at the University of North Texas has advice on team working at www.workteams.unt.edu. There are also some useful pointers on the Teams That Work website at www.teamsthatwork.co.uk.

- The *Nonverbal Dictionary Of Gestures, Signs & Body Language Cues* at http://members.aol.com/nonverbal2/diction1.htm offers information about non-verbal communication.

- To find out about employment rights and disciplinary procedures, visit the website of the UK Advisory, Conciliation and Arbitration Service at www.acas.org.uk.

- For information about health and safety at work, visit the Health and Safety Executive website at www.hse.gov.uk.

- The UK Department of Trade and Industry website offers advice on quality and continuous improvement at www.dti.gov.uk/quality/1i.htm. The website of Arizona State University gives guidance on continuous improvement tools at www.west.asu.edu/tqteam/resource.htm.

- The Free Management Library at www.managementhelp.org has information about all aspects of management, including communication, personal and career development and leadership.

- Many of the books that have been quoted in *Leading Teams* can help you to understand team leadership and develop your own skills. Three that are particularly worth reading are Ricardo Semler's *Maverick* (Random House: 2001); David Taylor's *The Naked Leader* (Capstone: 2002); and John Adair's *Effective Leadership* (Pan: 1988).

# Acknowledgments

You can find out more about the ideas referred to in *Leading Teams* from the original sources listed below, which are gratefully acknowledged.

## Chapter

**1**    page 3  The four definitions of teams on come, respectively, from:

- Jon Katzenbach and Douglas Smith, *The Wisdom of Teams* (McGraw-Hill Education: 1998)

- Donelson Forsyth, *Group Dynamics* (Brooks Cole: 1998)

- Richard Storch, in his web-based lecture series *Introduction to Manufacturing Systems* at the University of Washington in Autumn 2003

- *Collins English Dictionary* (HarperCollins: 1999).

**2**    page 9  R Meredith Belbin's team roles are described in *Management Teams: Why They Succeed or Fail* (Butterworth-Heinemann: 2003).

page 12  Marvin Bower made the comment about culture in *The Will to Manage: Corporate Success Through Programmed Management* (McGraw-Hill: 1966).

**3**    page 17  Ricardo Semler describes his unusual management style in *Maverick* (Random House: 2001).

**4**    page 19  Douglas McGregor described the two types of manager in *The Human Side of Enterprise,* first published in 1960. The 1987 edition is available from Penguin.

page 23  Bruce Tuckman described the 'forming, storming, norming, performing' model in the article 'Developmental sequence in small groups' (*The Psychological Bulletin* 63, pp.384-399: 1965).

page 24  Rover steps provided by John Hillier, Change Management Leader, Rover Body and Pressings, 1997.

**5**    page 27  The full mission statements can be found at:
http://www2.marksandspencer.com/thecompany/whoweare/index.shtml
http://www.epilepsyscotland.org.uk/index.asp?id=49
http://www.admin.cam.ac.uk/univ/mission.html
http://www.barlow.co.uk/docs/our_philosophy.html
http://www.btplc.com/Corporateinformation/Ourstrategy.htm

**6**     page 35  The source of the army traits is
http://www.nwlink.com/~donclark/leader/leadchr.html

page 36  The four strategies for leadership come from Warren Bennis and
Burt Nanus in *Leaders: Strategies for Taking Charge* (HarperBusiness:
1997).

page 36  The three sets of behaviours are described by John Kotter in
*Leading Change* (Harvard Business School Press: 1996).

page 37  James MacGregor Burns introduced the concepts of
transactional and transformational leadership in his book *Leadership*
(Harper & Row: 1978).

page 38  The list of leadership characteristics was drawn up by Lew
Perrin in 'An analysis of the conceptual building blocks of leadership',
Table 2, page 4 in *Comparing Entrepreneurship and Leadership* (Council for
Excellence in Management and Leadership: 2002).

**7**     page 40  John Adair first described action-centred leadership in *Action
Centred Leadership* (McGraw-Hill: 1973; Gower: 1987). The diagram is
based on one from this book.

**8**     p45/46  The leadership styles are based on Paul Hersey and Kenneth
Blanchard in *Management of Organizational Behavior* (Prentice-Hall: 1972).

**9**     page 52  David Taylor describes his approach to changing your own
behaviour in *The Naked Leader* (Capstone: 2002).

**14**    page 84  Abraham Maslow first published his ideas on motivation in
*Toward a Psychology of Being* in 1968 (3rd edition, John Wiley & Sons:
1998).

page 86  Frederick Herzberg's two factor theory first appeared in *The
Motivation to Work* (John Wiley: 1959).

page 87  Victor Vroom's theories were published in *Work and Motivation*
(John Wiley: 1964).

**16**    page 99  – see Chapter 2, page 12.

**18**    pages 110 and 111  The workplace accident statistics are based on *Health
and Safety Statistics 2001/02* (HSE Books: 2002).

**19**    page 117  David Mead was quoted in an interview with
eCustomerServiceWorld in July 2000.

**24**    page 144  The PDCA cycle made popular by Deming was originally
developed by Walter A Shewhart in 1939 in *Statistical Method From the
Viewpoint of Quality Control*. (Current edition Dover Publications: 1986).

# Index

Key words are shown in blue.

*Leading Teams* is printed on paper from sustainable forest reserves and is elemental chlorine free (EFC)

Editorial team | Claire Nash, Robyn West and Nicola Bull, VisàVis Publications

Design team | Sarah Dobinson and Suzanne Richards, Axiom Design

Printed by | Giltedge Printers Ltd.